T0031174

WHAT WE
BUILD
WITH POWER

THE FIGHT FOR ECONOMIC JUSTICE IN TECH

DAVID DELMAR SENTÍES

BEACON PRESS
BOSTON

BEACON PRESS
Boston, Massachusetts
www.beacon.org

Beacon Press books
are published under the auspices of
the Unitarian Universalist Association of Congregations.

26 25 24 23   8 7 6 5 4 3 2 1

This book is printed on acid-free paper that meets the uncoated paper
ANSI/NISO specifications for permanence as revised in 1992.

Text design and composition by Kim Arney

Library of Congress Cataloging-in-Publication Data is available for this title.

ISBN: 978-0-8070-0667-2
E-book: 978-0-8070-0668-9; audiobook: 978-0-8070-0833-1

To the Resilient Coders community.
May we all draw strength from each other
and return strength to each other.

To all the people in my life who've
modeled resilience, each in their own way.

CONTENTS

INTRODUCTION

IN 1815, HISTORY'S MOST CELEBRATED military playbook was written by a soldier reeling from defeat. Carl von Clausewitz had been among the Prussian men captured by Napoleon's forces following a humiliating invasion, after which he spent a year in captivity. It's believed that his time spent ruminating on that loss, playing and replaying different scenarios in his head, inspired his magnum opus. I am convinced that *At War* could only have been written from a place of frustration. It's frustration, rather than victory, that offers the greatest wisdom.

I'm no Clausewitz. And this is no magnum opus. But it is a howl of frustration.

I write these lines a few hours after having told a group of our students that pride is a complicated feeling. I was pumping them up for our Demo Day, at which they'll be presenting their capstone projects to an assembly of prospective employers. They're all talented young adults of color who have no background in tech but who have spent the last five months grinding their way through a nearly impossible bootcamp to become software engineers. They were frustrated with their own projects, because they weren't perfect. They were nervous, which I believe is a symptom of love. You don't get nervous when you don't care. They were anxious to get off the call with me and get back to work, debugging and reworking. These are all manifestations of the pride we take in our work.

I'm the founder of this bootcamp. And I'm immensely proud of it. In other words, I have an unholy mess of feelings about it. I spend just about all of my waking hours ruminating about what has worked, what hasn't, and what would need to change about the entire industry for us to be able to even approach the impact we set out to make. We cannot, by ourselves, execute our own mission to advance economic resilience in Black and Brown communities. Think about that for a second: We spend all of our time fighting for something we fundamentally cannot accomplish alone. In a sense, it means that we operate in a perpetual state of losing. We score some wins along the way, but we're losing. And we are proud.

Resilient Coders is a highly competitive coding bootcamp that exists for the express purpose of building economic resilience in communities of color. Everything we do is meant to serve this purpose. We're unapologetic, for example, about the inclusion of race in our mandate. We work with people of color, and about 90 percent of those people of color self-identify as Black or Latinx. All of our students live in economically precarious circumstances. Few of them have had the opportunity to graduate from college. We don't charge our students a dime—not before, during, or after the program. In fact, we pay them to learn, in order to offset the privilege of time enjoyed by other candidates for software engineering jobs. We staff up to support our students, maintaining a low student-to-instructor ratio and a dedicated nontechnical support team. We have a sales team that brings employers to the table, in order to try to propel our alumni over the barricades. Our pedagogy is rigorously human-centric. It's based on Brazilian educator Paulo Freire's *Pedagogy of the Oppressed*, which is to say that we subscribe to a model of education that is based on exploration among peers rather than the more traditional banking of facts. We conduct no standardized tests before, during, or at the end of the program, since they skew heavily White and male. We place our students exclusively into full-time jobs, as software engineers, with competitive salaries. We charge our employers a placement fee, because we fundamentally believe that the expense of workforce training must be assumed by entities other than the student if we're ever going to see a change in the industry.

Maybe the most important note to make about the program is that most of the decisions we've made in pursuit of our vision of a rigorously worker-centric approach to workforce training have jeopardized, at some point and at some level, our ability to grow or even maintain the business. We made them anyway. All of this is anti-systemic. We've done it, so far, in that Resilient Coders is alive and well. But it works by sheer force of will most of the time. And sometimes it doesn't work at all.

Just as this book was born of frustration, so was the organization. There are too few Latinxs in tech. And even among our small subset, most of us who've made it into good high-paying jobs tend to be White Latinxs, like me. I've been lucky in many ways. Most Latinxs in this country, especially those with African or Indigenous roots, live in a state of economic oppression, which was violently cultivated over centuries for the development of American industry. One of my frustrations with tech was, and remains, the tendency to decouple underrepresentation from a legacy of intentional economic oppression that persists today.

In 2014, I started by spending my vacation days from my job at PayPal volunteering at a youth detention center, teaching young men the fundamentals of web development on laptops without internet access. The head of education at the facility asked me what we should call my class. I didn't really know or care. I suggested we call it Coding 101.

She laughed at me. "Literally no one will attend that class," she said. "You need to give it a name that simultaneously says what the class is and also allows the boys to see themselves in it." Thus, the name Resilient Coders was spoken into existence, over the phone.

Eventually I was able to pull together a couple of grants that allowed me to quit my job and start experimenting with a business model. Seven years later, as I write this, we haven't stopped experimenting. Resilient Coders has been at least six different organizations so far and hopefully will become many more in the future. Each one of those pivots has been precipitated by the one question that sets us apart from other nonprofit workforce development programs. It's a short question but a complicated one. It's our team's greatest source of strife, turbulence, and motivation. It's our heart and soul. It's our persistent challenge, our greatest strength, and every mundane thought or reflection in between. In a word, it's our pride. How do we best show up for our students and their communities?

We challenge ourselves. We pivot. We rebuild something that's closer to our values, always pressing up against our financial capacity. The reality is that we make no money by hiring more support staff or by extending our stipends. With every advancement we make comes a second important question: Is this actually sustainable? Because becoming better at what you do, in the nonprofit world, doesn't necessarily mean an increase in revenue.

Fortunately for us, we've been able to continue growing as a business while we've improved the programming. We've gotten very good at being a coding bootcamp: typically, between 85 and 90 percent of our graduates go on to find jobs as full-time software engineers, with salaries averaging in the nineties. But then this brings us to a third important question. The whole point of the bootcamp is to build economic resilience in communities of color. I started this organization as a vehicle through which to fight for economic justice. To what degree is it actually working? It works very well at a relatively small scale. We're great at training people for jobs as software engineers and putting them into jobs at companies where hiring managers are interested in entertaining a conversation with an organization like Resilient Coders. There's not much we can do about the alum's experience on the job, other than to advocate to our point of contact, whose power to intervene in instances of poor or unjust management is usually limited. Skills training providers like us live with a certain cognitive dissonance. We know that it's too often the case for people of color that landing and keeping a job is not just about the skills. It's about the barriers they face in entering the workforce at a level that is commensurate with those same skills. The Libertarian dream that education transcends race is demonstrably untrue, as we'll unpack in these pages.

On one level is the explicit and overt racism that our alumni experience at their jobs. We used to keep a list titled "Racist shit employers do," which we would discuss with our company contacts. Sometimes they acted on what we told them, but mostly they didn't. Some people got fired, but in our experience, fewer people lose their jobs at the trigger end of racism than at the barrel end.

What do we do, as a skills training provider, considering the cultural context? What's our role? The one thing we are structurally designed to do is to train. So we do. We meet with our alum. We play whatever role the students need us to play in making them even stronger programmers. Sometimes we're running drills. Often, we're just cheering them on and encouraging them to get back out there and submit their résumés to companies that are probably going to exclude them as strenuously as the ones they just left. *Endure it* is our implicit message. *The pay is good.*

This complicates our relationship with our most important goal, to show up in meaningful ways for our students and their communities. Can we really do no better than "Get back out there"? The pandemic struck before we could focus our efforts on answering that question. Resilient Coders survived 2020 by the sheer force of will of our staff, our students, our alumni, our board, and a much bigger army of allies than I'd realized we had. Our champions showed up out of nowhere. Advocates were pushing their companies to hire from the program despite layoffs and hiring freezes. It worked: our 2020 graduates found jobs. It was during this year of Uprisings that we discovered a burgeoning subculture in tech: People were ready to mobilize. They'd been out in the streets in June, and they were bringing the protest with them into the workplace. It seemed like a turning point in a conversation about race and tech that had been languishing for years in a quagmire of performative gestures, statements, and LinkedIn posts. Momentum was building. We were determined to leverage it into a broader transformation of tech culture. It would start with a transformation of Resilient Coders. Another pivot.

It's not enough. It's not systemic. No systemic shift can happen without a cultural shift to pave the way, and the cultural shift has leveled out. Skills training is a small piece of a system, no matter the size or the reach of the organization. It's an important piece, but it's still fundamentally an umbrella standing against a gale. At some point we need to shift the direction of the wind.

In January we were generating ideas for the future of Resilient Coders, some of which are in this book. I wanted us to adopt an approach like worker centers, in which we engage in training but also in workplace advocacy. I believe we should establish a national network of organizations like ours and our collective alumni to delineate industry standards meant to protect the interests of the worker. I would argue that we need to find a sustainable way to pay for workforce development and free it from an overdependence on philanthropy without putting the expense back on the student. As long as the onus of paying for education is on the student, we will continue to see a yawning and unending stratification of wealth in America. And even if we do manage to enact all of these changes, there's still an elephant in the room: nothing will change at all in tech until tech culture materially changes.

All of this—even *one* of these ideas—is much bigger than Resilient Coders. We just can't do it without sacrificing or overstretching our ability to execute our mission. There's something to be said for hyper-focusing on one thing and doing it very well. Our students deserve our focus. So we run an exceptional bootcamp.

But we can't keep catapulting our graduates over the barricades forever. It doesn't make sense to turn a blind eye to the reasons for which we founded the bootcamp so that we can focus exclusively on the bootcamp. At some point we need to participate in the cultural shift that needs to happen before we can embark on any path to real systemic transformation.

Frustration can spiral down into despair, or it can catalyze hope. It's a choice. Clausewitz left Prussia in frustration after its treaty with France and returned to the field in a Russian uniform. He applied the lessons he'd learned from earlier losses to win a battle against a French army twice the strength of his own, keeping Napoleon isolated from his reinforcements at Waterloo. Defeat and frustration can be powerful conduits to victory.

This is a book written from a place of frustration but not of despair. I believe this fight is winnable. I don't have a playbook, really. Nor do I have some sort of linear strategy; I don't think such a thing is possible. Neither did Clausewitz, for what it's worth. He believed in preparing for, and leaning into, the turbulence and uncertainty in every situation, forever grounded in purpose. Purpose, to him, was everything.

I believe in our purpose. I have faith in our collective ability to realize it. This book is my shot in the dark. I wrote it for you. Share it.

CHAPTER 1

POWER CONSCIOUSNESS

A FREE SOCIETY is one in which people don't have to spend all their time working in order to survive. In fact, the presence of an entire class of people who need to give their lifetimes over to their labor just so they can continue to live is symptomatic of a society that is not free. The working poor, disproportionately Black and Latinx, deserve economic justice.

Meanwhile, the tech community is ostensibly confronting its "diversity" problem. It continues to fail to understand not only the roots of the diversity crisis but also the reasons why it really matters. As long as we're not talking about the systemic dynamics and imbalances of power—their history, as well as their persistence today—tech will continue to miss the point. We need to fundamentally transform tech culture.

Economic injustice doesn't happen by accident. Over the course of a single generation, the rules of how our society should function have been quietly rewritten, in favor of a privileged few, at the expense of most people. The increase in the gross domestic product (GDP) per capita over the last thirty years suggests that the economy has been growing, having risen over 60 percent. Corporate profits during this time, as a share of that growing

GDP, have skyrocketed from 6 percent to 9 percent. On paper, it would seem that America has spent thirty years in growth mode. Unfortunately, the same cannot be said for the prosperity of the American people. During this same period that GDP per capita was growing at 60 percent, the typical household saw an increase of only 16 percent. Going back more than forty years to 1980, after accounting for inflation and government subsidies, wages have been largely stagnant for American earners on the bottom half of the bell curve. In a generation, the standard of living has not risen at all for effectively *half* of all Americans.

It's been getting steadily worse. Nearly 90 percent of baby boomers (born beginning in the 1940s) outearned their parents. However, only 60 percent of people born in the 1970s outearned their parents. And only about half of Americans born in the 1980s are outearning their parents so far. Overall, we're experiencing a steady relative decline in wage growth.

While the ship is sinking around the middle and working classes, America's wealthy are hovering above the wreckage. Wages for the top 1 percent of earners have tripled during the past thirty years. For CEOs, they've jumped 900 percent.[1]

The chasm is widening. The economic repercussions of the COVID-19 pandemic have been either devastating or wonderful, depending on where you sit on the spectrum of wealth. The stock market, untethered from the realities of most Americans, has boomed. The Institute for Policy Studies notes that, as of May 2022, American billionaires have seen a combined surge in their wealth of nearly 37 percent, or $1.7 trillion during the quarantine. Entrepreneur Elon Musk's wealth has increased more than tenfold during the pandemic, to $255 billion.[2] Meanwhile, employment for the lowest-wage workers plummeted 14 percent between January and July 2020. Recovery for these workers has been the most sluggish, predictably, as many pandemic furloughs became permanent layoffs.[3] While the employment rate for high-wage workers was still down 8.5 percent in April 2022, the low-wage employment rate was down 24 percent.[4]

This is disastrous for almost everyone in this country who is not a billionaire, which, unfortunately, is most of us. But as with most American manifestations of inequality, people of color are the hardest hit. The crisis of inequality is not just classist. It's racialized.

Acknowledging the relationship between race and poverty is uncomfortable for White people, and so it's routinely omitted from public discourse on poverty. One of our mainstream political parties, eager to attract the votes of the White working class during a period of inflamed racial tensions, has constructed a mythology in which people of color are simultaneously less deserving of federal aid than White people and more dependent on it. Neither is true. At Resilient Coders, our free nonprofit coding bootcamp, we've been offered money to assert that race plays no role in our admissions process. We made no such assertion and received no money. The instant poverty becomes agnostic about race, so will we.

In contemporary America, a person's race is inextricably tied to their ability to build wealth, because Black and Indigenous people simply face greater systemic challenges as a whole than others do. White people have never been systematically and explicitly prohibited from developing intergenerational wealth. This has been a common trope throughout the history of nonwhite people in America, and one that persists today. But that's a topic for another book.

Stark racial disparities appear even among the impoverished. White poverty and Black poverty, for example, are simply not the same. Recent data indicate that impoverished White families hold, on average, $18,000 in wealth, while impoverished Black families are closer to zero.[5] This statistic in itself is staggering, even before we consider the implication that half of those Black families must have a net worth that is less than zero.

I live in Boston, the supposed beacon of progressive values, which also hosts the greatest wealth inequalities in the entire country. The White household median net worth here is $247,500. And among Black families, it's $8.[6] For Dominicans it's $0. Are White people really working thirty-one thousand times harder than Black people? Or is deep injustice at work here?

We are not prepared for automation.

I'd argue that there is deep injustice, and that it's about to get deeper, as the onset of automation threatens many of the jobs on which entire communities depend. The streets of my neighborhood are lined with cars with Uber and Lyft stickers on their windshields. They belong mostly to Black and Latino men working hard for meager wages and no benefits, for these last few remaining years before their jobs are automated. The more hours they log, the more of their money is sent to Uber and Lyft, which then invest that capital in the technology that will ultimately displace their workforce.

The problem isn't just in the ride-sharing industry, and it's not confined to our urban hubs. There is also a disproportionate number of Black people employed as truck drivers hauling cargo, "roughly 156,000 more . . . than their total numbers in the US population would predict."[7] When truck driving by people disappears, it will impact everyone, but it will impact Black families the most.

The COVID-19 pandemic has accelerated the eradication of jobs that were already vulnerable to automation. *Time* reports that many of the jobs that disappeared in 2020 are probably gone for good, with estimates as high as 42 percent of jobs lost.[8] The automation of jobs became an instrument of public health: Machines don't get sick. They can continue mopping floors at airports. They can keep patrolling shuttered malls, recording your takeout orders at restaurants, ringing up your groceries, and fielding your customer service calls. Automation allowed businesses to stay open during a time when it was unsafe for people to go to a worksite outside the home. Necessity spurred the adoption of technology, as it has for millennia. Just as many of us adopted platforms such as Zoom to continue working safely, other business owners adopted various technological solutions to stay afloat through these challenging years as well.

And why should they go back to the way things were? If you own a neighborhood restaurant, already operating on slim margins, and are still recovering from the pandemic, do you really box up your Roomba and set it in the storage closet so that you can pay someone to sweep the floors at the end of every shift? Now that your customers have gotten used to placing their takeout orders through the Toast app, do you really delete your account and reconnect your landline? If some of your vendors have managed to use software that reduces their staffing costs and are passing on those savings to you in order to retain your business, do you really stick with the more expensive vendors, as a matter of principle? Or do you fight for your small business, and the family that depends on it, by reducing your overhead?

The answers are clear, and this is why the idea that we can resist automation requires a position of privilege that most people don't have. Most of us need to save money. Automation is not something that can be prevented. It's an inevitability of the economic system in which we operate. We can choose how we respond to it and the degree to which we adopt or embrace it. But we can't afford to ignore it, nor do we enjoy the luxury of harboring illusions of fighting it. You're better off riding the train than standing on the tracks in protest.

The problem is that those train tickets are hard to come by. Not even office jobs are safe, and race is as much a factor in the white-collar economy as it is in the working class. Black people are statistically much more likely than White people to play the supportive roles that are vulnerable to automation. These are jobs such as assistants and office managers, as opposed to directors and managers of people. The wage growth associated with supportive roles has already been slowing down, relative to director roles, even before the recent acceleration of automation.

Just as Black people are overrepresented in the jobs that will succumb to automation, they are underrepresented in the jobs that will thrive in the automation economy. Just as there are 156,000 too many Black truck drivers relative to their proportion of the US population, there are about 100,000 too few Black software engineers.

The solution seems simple when stated simply: Let's teach those truck drivers how to code. We can pull people out of automation-vulnerable careers and put them into automation-resilient careers. They make more money, tech solves its talent crisis, and the economy gets an adrenaline shot as thousands of Americans transition to a sector of the economy that seems to be endlessly expanding. Everybody wins. Right?

Unfortunately, that is an overly simplistic solution, for a number of reasons, not least because not everybody wants to be or should be a programmer. But it's also overly simplistic culturally. It reinforces the myth of meritocracy endemic to White-dominant American culture. It's an echo of a persistent narrative that anyone who tries hard enough can get ahead, if they just have the grit and gumption. Conversely, so the narrative goes, if you can't get ahead, it's your own fault.

The myth of meritocracy has a long history in America. It's best understood alongside its sister myth, that of the democratization of our institutions. We love to "democratize" arenas in America and celebrate the notion that we're in a constant state of blowing open doors and broadening access to everything for everyone. The myth of college as a democratizing institution— the idea that if a young person is smart enough and ambitious enough, she can go to college and realize her full professional potential regardless of circumstance—is a particularly harmful example. It's perpetuated by those who have been academically and professionally successful, because we all want to believe that our gains have been won in a fair fight.

So goes one of the great ironies of American culture: our "democratizing" institutions are for sale, thereby subverting their democratizing influence. And it is their supposed democratizing influence that makes them worth buying in the first place.

Meritocracy is up for sale.

Among the many causes of our crisis of economic injustice is the deterioration of the social contract between industry, government, and education. Starting with the Franklin Roosevelt administration in the 1930s, there existed for a time a collaborative effort across those three institutions to put Americans to work. Employers wanted employees who were adequately trained. Workforce training services performed that training. Government served the function of convening, scaling, and sustaining this pipeline. This model worked, through America's postwar manufacturing boom. College acted as a conduit to a certain segment of the workforce but certainly was not necessary to sustain a comfortable middle-class existence.

The economy's shift from manufacturing to services over the course of the latter half of the twentieth century has meant an increase in the number of jobs for which a college education is required. This shift launched a degree inflation phenomenon, with more and more job requisitions asking for a bachelor's degree—and often even a master's degree—for jobs that fundamentally do not require any level of higher education to perform. Degree inflation has accelerated since the recession of 2008, with 99 percent of jobs created requiring some sort of post-secondary credentialing, which is accessible to only half of Americans.[9]

And it gets worse: Many companies are now hiring almost exclusively from expensive private universities. So, essentially, besides requiring a bachelor's degree, they are also implicitly requiring that the bachelor's degree be expensive and unattainable to the overwhelming majority of Americans.

It's important to point out that many tech jobs should not require a degree, as an increasing number of technologists will tell you. HackerRank CEO Vivek Ravisankar notes, in the *2018 Student Developer Report*, that "self-directed learning is the norm among developers; so when companies focus on hiring based on proven skill instead of prestigious degree or GPA, a massive pool of overlooked talent opens up."[10] Of the ten thousand developers HackerRank surveyed for the report, nearly a third reported being entirely self-taught.

In programming specifically, the languages, frameworks, and libraries that are actually used on the job are not necessarily the same as those taught in college. This is a function of the reality that the industry changes faster than syllabi can keep up. According to a report I ran using Lightcast, a labor data aggregator, there are roughly the same number of entry-level jobs posted in a given year requiring proficiency in Java as there are for jobs requiring proficiency in JavaScript. They sound similar, but Java and JavaScript are two completely different programming languages, seldom overlapping in the same job requisition. Java is taught in college. JavaScript is usually not. It's commonly assumed on campus that you'll simply teach yourself JavaScript, especially now, given the proliferation of online resources to help you learn it. Significantly, the Lightcast report shows similar salaries for jobs requiring the skill learned in college and jobs requiring the skill you're supposed to teach yourself. Imagine paying off your massive student debt with the skills you taught yourself.

Thanks to a booming demand for talent, a growing number of companies are dropping their computer science degree requirements, as a way of expanding the tops of their funnels. For them, the new frontier will mean accounting for the privilege of time: the fact that some students are able to teach themselves the popular new languages and frameworks between classes and work on the cool side projects that recruiters want to see, while their less privileged classmates are in the cafeteria washing dishes.

The other, much more insidious repercussion of the growing dominance of college as a prerequisite to certain careers is the perpetuation of the myth of meritocracy. Too many of the empowered are allowed to believe that their advantage is entirely legitimate, that they earned it by attending college. And that if only more people could attend college, our high-growth industries would employ a workforce as diverse as the cities that host them. This is a popular myth because it simultaneously absolves the empowered of guilt, passively acknowledges the structural racism that the empowered know they are supposed to acknowledge, and neatly presents a conclusion they believe is plausible.

The myth of meritocracy requires a deep faith in college as our civilization's great leveling force. You'd have to make yourself believe that it's a mechanism with limitless and diverse input and with output distinguishable only by talent, irrespective of race and class. In short, you'd have to believe that college is a democratic and democratizing institution.

If this was ever true, it's not true today. College has become our new aristocracy, with parental wealth being directly linked to a student's academic success.[11] In their book *The Merit Myth: How Our Colleges Favor the Rich and Divide America*, Anthony Carnevale, Peter Schmidt, and Jeff Strohl observe that "higher education serves to compound the advantages and disadvantages that people had as children."[12] This is evident at all points of advancement, from getting accepted into college to graduating and getting a job.

The wealth and socioeconomic status of a student's parents are so important to the student's success through college that they eclipse her actual talent. If the student has low test scores, but her parents are among the top socioeconomic quartile, she has a 70 percent chance of graduating from college with a bachelor's degree or higher. If she has top test scores, but her parents are among the lower socioeconomic quartile, her chances of graduating from college with a bachelor's degree or higher are 30 percent.[13] Talent matters; privilege matters more.

Getting through the admissions process and into college is difficult enough for students from low-income families. Paying for it is nearly impossible. The cost of tuition has ballooned out of control and created a massive crisis of student loan debt in America. It's not an accident. There is a reason for these rampant increases, as we'll unpack later in this book.

In the year 2000, we had in the US, collectively, $200 billion in student loans. In 2012, we hit $1 trillion. And as I write this, in 2020, we've reached $1.7 trillion, with the average college student graduating with $32,000 of debt.[14] This financial commitment is wildly out of reach for the average American, who cannot produce $500 in a medical emergency. For the impoverished, this is not even remotely an option.

College costs have a deep impact on our economy, as the Federal Reserve Bank of Boston notes in a 2019 study.[15] Crippled by student loan payments, fewer young people are buying homes, and we're forestalling our family planning, since we can't afford to have children. I'm a millennial. My own generation is too late for the American Dream. And it will likely be worse for the next generation.

────────

Attitudes regarding policy proposals that would make college free are deeply racialized. Black and Latinx Americans support them at 86 percent and 82 percent, respectively. Non-Hispanic White people support these proposals at 53 percent. The most virulently opposed are those who most benefited from affordable college: older White Republicans.[16] After having reaped the harvest sown by their parents and grandparents, they want to torch the field.

Defenders of college as a democratic and democratizing institution will rally around the idea that an accomplished student can get a scholarship or financial aid. Assistance is available. Unfortunately, that assistance is offered to the privileged. In the scramble for students from wealthy families, colleges are increasingly offering financial aid to those who don't need it, in order to sway the family's decision in their favor. It's not a bad investment: those scholarships might beget endowments.[17] And those students will spend differently on campus. Colleges have no economic incentive to actually occupy the democratizing role that they do in our mythology. No, it takes more than talent and ambition to go to college.

Then there's the question of what qualifies as "achievement" to a college admissions office. Typically, admissions officers are looking for indicators of class, such as the prestige of a student's high school, the extracurricular activities they were able to do, the unpaid internships and volunteer work, and whether the student is somehow already networked into that college's community. These "achievements" are harder to come by for young people from low-income families.

The notion that an accomplished student can get into college with scholarships and financial aid is popular because it allows us to blame the oppressed for their oppression. If they're poor, it's because of poor education. If they have received poor education, it's because they couldn't go to college. And if they couldn't go to college, it's because they weren't smart enough to get scholarships. Or their families don't value education. It's important to the victor to believe that his fight was fairly won. It's his legitimacy. And that legitimacy is worth buying.

Many of those accomplished students from low-income families do go to college and find that it's *still* not enough to launch high-paying and high-growth careers. College is not necessarily preparing them for the workforce. A huge proportion of college graduates—particularly women, people of color, and really just about anyone without a degree in a STEM field—will be underemployed at their first job, earning significantly less than is appropriate for their level of skill, training, or experience. This has lifelong economic repercussions. The Strada Institute, in partnership with Burning Glass Technologies, argues in their report *The Permanent Detour* that grads who begin their careers underemployed will stay underemployed for a long time. That includes a whopping 47 percent of female college graduates and 37 percent of their male classmates. Those who started their careers underemployed are five times more likely to remain underemployed relative to their classmates five years after graduating. And then, five years after that, *three-quarters* of those who were underemployed during years one and five of their employment remain underemployed after a decade.[18]

There are college graduates who manage to escape underemployment: those whose first job is in computer science. They have a 51 percent chance of getting back on track. Those whose first job is in office or administrative support have a 39 percent chance of getting back on track. The fields in which people of color tend to be overrepresented, particularly grounds maintenance, transportation, and food service, offer their college-educated workforce a 25 percent chance of escaping underemployment.[19] Earning a bachelor's degree is not the surefire path to prosperity that we like to pretend it is.

Far from being the great leveling force of our civilization, higher education serves to exacerbate existing inequalities. We see this all the time at Resilient Coders among our applicants. The overwhelming majority of folx who apply to Resilient Coders have attempted college but had to drop out for financial reasons. Either the tuition was too high, or they couldn't be without a full-time paycheck for four years. They might have had a campus job, but it didn't pay nearly enough to live on, particularly in cities with rapidly increasing costs of living. Even in the extremely rare instance in which college is absolutely free, people still cannot afford the time it takes to go to college. They have to work to survive.

We see patterns in our Resilient Coders admissions interviews. We have the student who attempted college with a combination of financial aid, scholarships, and debt, hoping that they might get more scholarships in future years. This attempt fails, for reasons that have nothing to do with academic performance, and the person drops out with debt and no degree. There is another version of a similar situation in which the person did drop out because of poor academic performance, caused by a diversion of their attention to a family emergency or trauma. Either a parent becomes ill, and the family cannot afford proper care, or someone is facing displacement, perhaps through eviction or deportation. The student drops out of college to get a job and see the family through the crisis.

Threat of deportation is a big factor in Resilient Coder applicants dropping out of college. Immigration policies are sold to the voting public as an effort to keep the impoverished from stretching our government subsidy programs, but they ironically kneecap immigrants' ability to thrive in this country, thereby forcing them into the same subsidy programs.

The archetype we're seeing more often at Resilient Coders is the high school student who's done the math on their odds and doesn't see the point of going into debt to obtain a college degree. They know people who've gotten bachelor's degrees. They see those friends and family members in low-wage jobs, without much of a shot at upward mobility, working long hours to pay off the debt they incurred to launch their careers. To the calculating high school student, watching the national personal debt crisis play out in the lives of their friends and family members, the myth of college as the door to the American Dream is a hard one to believe. That's not what they see. They see their older siblings unable to buy a home because of their student loans. They hear about ruined credit scores. They're watching their parents work ever harder in order to put a kid through college. We have a Resilient Coders alum whose father struck a deal with a college, agreeing to perform janitorial services in order to work off some of his kid's tuition.

And for what? So that the most heavily indebted generation of Americans can enter a weak job market and do work that does not leverage the skills they learned but that still somehow requires the degree?

"It doesn't matter what the degree is in." The recruiter I spoke to from one of the enterprises that was interested in hiring from Resilient Coders spelled it out for me. "As long as they have the degree." In other words, the actual content of the instruction being delivered in college doesn't matter at all. The fact that someone is being educated, or not educated, in a certain subject matter is not as important as the fact that, at some point, someone somewhere paid for the education. Imagine buying something expensive just so you can later tell someone that you bought it. Whether the product actually performs the function written on the box doesn't matter. Really, what you're buying, as you count out the $200,000, is the receipt.

In the end, though, the receipt does have value.

The recruiter was mollified when we offered an alum who happened to have a theology degree from a seminary. The young man was certified to celebrate Catholic mass, which granted him an interview for a software engineering role. The theology degree conferred on our alum an advantage that he would not have otherwise had. College, like the dollar, derives much of its value from a popular consensus that it has value. Our student was not presented with any assessment confirming his mastery of theology. The talent acquisition team was not interested in scrutinizing the quality of the education our alum had received, just in knowing that he had, in fact, received it. It was enough that he was among the educated, standing on the right side of a velvet rope to which we've collectively assigned this role of demarcation. Us and them.

I had the privilege of going to a great art school and, during my studies, enjoyed a period of intellectual and artistic growth. But that was never the real reason I felt compelled to go to college. I didn't go into debt so that I could explore the difference between Classical Greek sculpture and Hellenistic sculpture. Fun though that was, it wasn't worth many thousands of dollars. I went into debt in the hopes of securing my spot in the middle class. I went to college so that I could get the first job that would set me on a path toward not having to worry about money. That was the return I expected on my investment. For me to have become an unemployed expert on Greek sculpture would have represented a failed investment. Like most Americans, I did not have the privilege of regarding education as its own reward. My landlord wasn't accepting art as rent payment.

The tech industry takes this elitism a step further. It's not enough to have the bachelor's degree; it needs to have been expensive. The industry suffers from a debilitating obsession with inaccessible private colleges *because* of their inaccessibility. As is the case with any commercial product, the brand has a value of its own. Brand is a communication of class. If you don't have it, you're not welcome. Nobody's hiring from state schools or community colleges.

This phenomenon is so hard to ignore in Boston that the New England Venture Capital Association launched an effort called Hack.Diversity to connect computer science graduates of local public colleges with technical jobs. Hack has evolved and grown since its founding in 2017 to include project-based continued technical upskilling. But the impetus for their founding was their frustration that Black and Brown engineers with degrees in computer science from public institutions were being passed over for jobs for which they were duly qualified. The existence of Hack. Diversity, like that of Resilient Coders, only makes sense in the context of the structural racism and classism endemic to the tech industry. In a truly meritocratic society in which having the skills is enough to get the job, there would be no chasm. We would need no bridge. Unfortunately, that's not the case.

It's worth noting that Hack has added another component to its program beyond the technical upskilling. They're also requiring employers to engage in accountability efforts through regular performance reviews with the Hack team to ensure that the lived experiences of their fellows match the company's stated values. The future of workforce development is accountability and advocacy.

As a part of my job at Resilient Coders, I often found myself addressing groups of technologists. I used to begin my speeches with an exercise: I'd ask everyone in the room to raise their hands if they work in tech. All the hands would go up. I'd ask people to keep them up if they were born and raised in Boston. Nearly all the hands would drop. Occasionally one or two hands would stay up. This exercise illustrated the fact that Boston's people are shut out of Boston's industry, which is both morally and economically indefensible. And there's a racial dynamic to this phenomenon. Only 28 percent of Black or US-born Latinx Bostonian workers have a college degree.[20] And those who do get degrees often earn them at a public institution, which—even when a degree is in a tech field—is often not enough to get a job in tech. Few attendees at these conferences, if any, have a degree, for instance, from the University of Massachusetts in Boston.

I eventually stopped doing this exercise, because it was predictable. No one was surprised.

Imagine being the first in your family to go to college, only to discover that your particular college holds no sway in the industry of your dreams. Your parents tightened their belts for years, saving for your tuition. You outperformed your classmates in high school. You took a job on nights and weekends, you took out the loans, you cobbled together the scholarships, you washed dishes in the college cafeteria, you put in the late nights at the keyboard, you skipped out on the parties, and you ended the friendships that were holding you back. You prayed, you bargained, and you wept. You showed up for your niece who looks up to you. And after the tearful graduation party at your parents' house, the words of admiration from your siblings and the words of hope from your grandparents, you find yourself in a brightly lit conference room with a recruiter who tells you that, at his company, in their engineering department, they usually don't hire from state schools. But there's a position in customer service, and the company culture is *awesome*.

"I mean, most of the engineers here are MIT grads," the recruiter tells you. Because—and here's the part that keeps you up at night—the job is "hard." In other words, it's not appropriate for you. You're not up to the task. Try something else. Something easier. Imagine communicating this message to your parents when they ask how the job search is going.

Demanding that someone have a degree in order to work in a position that does not require the knowledge conferred by that degree to perform is a legally permissible way to discriminate based on someone's or someone's parents' ability to pay for college. Most tech companies are taking this a step further, requiring implicitly that the degree also be expensive.

Everything about the college-to-workforce pipeline serves to exacerbate disparities in wealth and power, not ameliorate them. Acceptance is itself an act of culling. The payment of tuition, the accessing of loans, the acquisition of financial aid, the allocation of a student's time are all opportunities for systemic discrimination. College is not one single act of segregation but rather a long series of discrete gears in an elaborate threshing machine.

There are those who want to fix this system. But it doesn't need to be fixed; it's not broken. It's functioning exactly as intended. It needs to be dismantled and rebuilt, to serve an entirely different purpose.

Broadening access to college is not enough. We don't need to make college a little bit more affordable or to consider forgiving a fraction of someone's student debt. These are incremental solutions, inadequate for a crisis of this magnitude. It's not about mentorship, nor is it about adding a few more scholarships or about increasing public funds for community colleges. Even if we were to somehow double the graduation rate of the top students from families in the bottom socioeconomic quartile, that would bring them only to a 60 percent chance of graduating from college. Those are the top students. Their odds, doubled, are still below those enjoyed by the worst students from privileged families, 70 percent. In this utopian vision, in which we've doubled the graduation rates for top students, we're still operating within a system in which wealth matters more than talent. We will just have succeeded in forcing a few more outliers through that system. That's not a solution. It's an adaptation to a system that remains oppressive and unchanged, which is different. Let's not confuse limping for healing.

The conduit through which Americans enter the automation-resilient workforce is broken and getting worse. It needs to be entirely reinvented. Until that happens, we need to build an alternate path.

A system worthy of being overcome is worthy of being overhauled.

A few years ago, some friends and I found ourselves at a bar with a former middle school classmate I hadn't seen in decades. We were in Boston's Seaport district, an overdeveloped commercial zone, enjoying craft beers in a trendy place situated within a two-mile stretch of land between the financial district and a row of commercial drydocks. There are chain stores in this area now. There is a bowling alley, a movie theater, and luxury high-rise condos where there had been a chapel and empty lots just a few years prior. You see no homeless people in this part of the city. There are no shelters, no community resources, and essentially no subsidized housing, as developers have generally sidestepped the requirements to build affordable units by allocating them elsewhere in the city. This was the setting in which our conversation turned to the economic realities that make Boston the most unequal city in the country, by distribution of wealth.

"Anyone can overcome the system," said my former classmate cheerily. She waved it off. She dismissed, with a literal wave of her hand, the entire notion of systemic poverty.

What was most striking about her deeply misguided comment was that she seemed to mean it as a compliment to me. She was celebrating Resilient Coders, riffing on my position that anyone can become a software engineer. There exist no innate distinctions between us, she was saying; given the chance, anyone can succeed. The system works more completely now, thanks to Resilient Coders. That's the idea.

I hear this a lot. I get some version of it from well-intentioned allies, who see us as plumbers restoring a leaky pipeline to its correct and optimal performance. The idea is that as long as there's some sort of conduit through which some number of brilliant outliers can achieve success, then the system is working as it should. This is a vision of a world in which some people follow the "conventional" track, others follow an "alternate" track that might be harder and narrower, but as long as we continue to see a trickle of hardscrabble Alexanders Hamilton make it to the other side, then it works. Both tracks converge at the endpoint.

I can see why people might think that and why they want to normalize the outliers. All we see in American culture is the outlier narrative.

"Anyone can overcome the system" is not an idea; it's a folksy aphorism. It's a mantra. It's a guiding principle, a cornerstone of Americanism. It's an opiate we swallow to avoid clarity. It's so deeply ingrained in our culture and in our sense of self that we've adopted it into our collective "common sense," as though it were true. As though the thirty-four million Americans living below the poverty line are all lazy, stupid, or both. Don't they know that anyone can overcome the system?

We need to start from scratch, with new objectives that reflect a clear-eyed view of reality.

What would it look like for us to have a system that equitably supports talented people rather than pushes against them? Is such a thing possible?

Suppose we start with this core tenet: *the process of entering and moving through the workforce should be fair.*

Fairness here means that a person's success along their professional trajectory is unaffected by their race, religion, gender identity or expression, class, socioeconomic status, or political affiliation. It means that they are judged on the basis of their merits. They advance through their careers based on how well they perform at work. A just workforce is actually meritocratic.

There is no reason to expect anything other than proportional representation in a fair and just system: in a city in which roughly half of the population is White, as is the case in Boston, roughly half the tech workforce would be White, just as half of the people incarcerated in our prisons would be White, and half of our impoverished population would be White.

There are employers who display a more meritocratic attitude in their recruitment and advancement of talent. They tell me they would hire anyone with the right skills, no matter who they are, where they're from, and whether they have a degree. This is a step in the right direction, one that moves quite a bit beyond most companies. But it's not quite far enough. These employers are deferring discrimination rather than confronting or eliminating it. Because who is it that has those "right skills" and why? Is it the guy who went to an expensive university and who was able to spend most of his time learning rather than working? Who is it that already knows the programming languages and frameworks they don't teach in college but are expected on the job? Is it the student who was able to hang out in her dorm room after class and work on unpaid personal projects? Is it the person who grew up with an awareness of software engineering as a potential and accessible career path, and started learning in high school? Is it the person who went to math camp in middle school? Was it the unpaid internships in college that clinched the deal? Is it the kid who grew up with a roster of future professional contacts, who would serve first as examples, then mentors, and now as connectors, eager to plug them into the industry of their choice? Is it the young people who've been walking a path that's been lit for them by others for years?

Certainly, competency-based hiring is an important component in a meritocratic workforce. But it's not a solution in itself. It's not a *system* so much as it is a single gear. By the time an employer is presented with two candidates and has to pick one, the dream of comparing apples to apples is already impossible.

So then what should employers do? Are they responsible for leveling the playing field between the two candidates? Is it on them to shoulder the burden of a broken educational system that coddled one and failed the other? The employer has a team to look out for, a product to ship, deadlines and milestones to hit, and a competitor to beat. Who pays for any additional training this new person might need? Who picks up the slack when they don't deliver or when a more seasoned employee spends time coaching and mentoring the newest addition to the team? Is this practice sustainable? And is it fair?

None of these challenges is insurmountable. There is not just one model addressing these concerns but a robust field of competing prototypes, some of which are identified in this book. As is the case in any field, some models are better than others. There are niches developing and variations being pioneered. There are other coding bootcamps like ours, as well as IT programs, state-sponsored apprenticeships with tax incentives, informal apprenticeships, cooperatives, and more. The question of how an employer might hire a candidate whose path has been less "traditional" than those of the other candidates has been answered repeatedly, over the course of years, by a long string of organizations, public entities, and progressive enterprises.

Let's ask a more fundamental question instead: What would a meritocratic workforce look like? Imagine, for the sake of the thought exercise, that we have no constraints and that we need not account for any budgetary considerations. What is the impossible, euphorically optimistic ideal?

Poverty would not obstruct a candidate's entrance into a truly meritocratic workforce. This means that the education necessary to get the job is free, and freely accessible. A student is paid to learn, such that they can drop a job to focus on their studies. There is no expectation that someone has been able to work for free, ever. No preference is given to the candidate with the unpaid internships; in fact, unpaid internships do not exist. No unpaid work is assigned by a prospective employer as a part of the interview process. The ability to build passion projects or contribute to open source applications is not limited to those with the privilege of free time.

A candidate's network, or lack thereof, does not affect their shot at a good job in a meritocratic workforce. Employee referrals stop immediately, to be continued once our personal networks are as diverse and pluralistic as our cities.

In a meritocratic workforce, the training is relevant to the career. Free education is not enough. It must actually prepare someone for the existing workforce. A waste of time is still a waste of money, even if no currency is exchanged.

There is a tendency at some companies to concentrate their efforts at a meritocratic workforce exclusively within a certain salary band. They partner with nonprofit workforce development organizations and agree to hire people with "nontraditional" backgrounds but only into low-wage jobs. They set up finite internships, often at an IT help desk, which pay $16 an hour, and in which workers have no chance at upward mobility. It's not that these folx are on the bottom rung of a tall ladder. It's that they are at the top of a step stool, with nowhere to go but back down.

Unfortunately, this approach is often supported by a huge community of nonprofit organizations that should be aiming higher. They might be operating under the conviction that any job is better than no job or with an overabundance of faith in the opportunities for upward mobility in tech. In reality, they're often commuting workers from underemployment in retail to underemployment in tech. Students engage in these programs, lured by promises of growth that seldom materialize. The people at these nonprofit programs see their responsibilities as fulfilled once their graduates land that first job in tech. After that, as a graduate of one such program told me, "Getting the second job is up to us." She got that second job. But she had to attend another program and learn a completely different set of skills to get it.

We must do better than giving students step stools and calling them ladders. In a truly meritocratic workforce, wages can support families, and jobs are not immediately vulnerable to automation. People have an opportunity to rise along with their property values, in proportion to their work ethic.[21] Our homes get more expensive over the years—so should we. People must be allowed, encouraged, and empowered to advance within a company if appropriate higher-level positions exist and to move beyond it if those positions do not exist.

Most employers seem unwilling to consider the opportunities for advancement in both on-the-job training and in thorough onboarding, which serve more than just the immediate purpose of upskilling a new employee. It allows employers to hire from a much broader pool of applicants, once they disabuse themselves of the expectation that someone should have the exact technical competencies that the job requires. Employers who think on-the-job training takes too long are missing the forest for the trees. The amount of time it takes one engineer to get caught up with the rest of the team is one variable in a complex system. And programmers should know better than to focus on a single variable.

This isn't altruism. Progressive companies sand down the advantages that the "traditional" candidates may have over the "nontraditional" ones, and in the process they break open a much broader pool of applicants, making it possible to select on the basis of attributes that you can't train for. No amount of college can make you more or less dependable, curious, resilient, or ambitious. These characteristics are what companies that are good at hiring are looking for. Mastering a framework, on the other hand, takes a few dozen hours at the keyboard and some coffee.

Insisting on hiring for specific technical competencies is like buying a house because you like the paint color. It's such an easy thing to change with a little bit of time. You'd be better served inspecting the infrastructure. What is the house really made of, and can it bear weight?

Advancement might also involve dedicating a certain number of hours per week to continued professional development. At the onset of someone's career, this could involve starting in a position that serves as a stepping-stone to the one they really want. For example, someone who wants to be a software engineer might start in Quality Assurance, with the expectation that they might make the move in a year. But such a plan requires a certain degree of intentionality. There is no shortage of companies that promise advancement without making any sort of commitment or putting a process in place. There's a vague reference to a meritocracy culture and a verbal promise that anyone who does well can advance to wherever they want to go. That might work for cisgender straight able-bodied White people, given that they have a shot at advancement that is commensurate with their level of skill. That's not the case for everyone.

In a meritocratic workforce, advancement is objective. And objectivity requires the clear communication of expectations and some degree of accountability. At Resilient Coders, we coach our employers to be objective by crafting a plan together. It's a clearly delineated description of what success looks like, throughout the period of advancement. For example, a company might decide that they need to hire on a temp-to-permanent basis. The idea is that if the candidate's tenure as a temp is successful—whatever that might mean—they will convert to full-time employment. We want to know what a successful first week on the job looks like. Then the second week. Third week. Month. Second month. Third month. Fourth month. If the worker hits those milestones, they must then convert to full-time employment. If the milestones are hit, but the company doesn't feel like they can hire the person full-time, there has been a failure on the part of the employer to communicate their expectations. We like removing ambiguity.

We practice what we preach at Resilient Coders. New employees get a monthly breakdown of what specific and objective indicators will denote success through each of their first three months with us. We check in weekly. At the end of those three months, we decide whether or not to keep them, based on their performance against those clearly stated performance indicators. During this three-month trial, they're receiving their full salary and benefits.

A meritocratic workforce is freely accessible to all. People advance through their careers on the basis of their sweat and their skill.

So who, or what, is precluding us from building a meritocratic workforce?

CHAPTER 2

WORKFORCE DEVELOPMENT AS A RADICAL ACT OF ECONOMIC LIBERATION

ONE OF THE GREAT THREATS to the struggle for economic liberation is that we don't all agree on what the word "liberation" actually means. Is it the absence of impositions by an external agency like a federal government? Is it about creating an environment in which there's a set of virtues, and those who abide by them achieve success? If so, what are those virtues, and who chooses them? And if I have to adopt your virtues in order to realize my own liberation, is that liberation? Or is that just a different form of imposition by an external agent? We'd have to begin the conversation by identifying a single shared understanding of what liberation means and how to quantify the extent to which it's accessible to all.

The philosopher Martin Hägglund describes liberty as the capability to pursue self-actualization. It's the ability to spend our lifetime doing the things that make us the people we want to be. Life is valuable, he argues, because it's finite. Time is short, and it can never be recovered, and so as much of it as possible should be spent in a way that we find fulfilling. "To sustain your existential identity," he writes, "is to lead your life in light of what you value."[1] Freedom is the ability to sustain that existential identity. It means having more time than that which you need to survive. The more time you have to live your life in light of what you value, the freer you are. Your free time is your free self.

If "freedom" means having the time necessary to live in a way that supports our "existential identity," then a free society is one in which people don't have to spend all of their time working in order to survive. In a free society, a full-time job grants each person a reliable source of income that allows them to live comfortably in their city, participate in its economy, and enjoy a fair amount of free time, with which they can do whatever it is that makes them more "them." Members of a free society have choice. They have agency over the way in which they spend their lifetime.

A free society is, by definition, one that values, promotes, and enables the freedom of its citizens. Free access to good jobs is a hallmark of such a society. But as long as access to good jobs is up for sale, restricting access for certain people remains a necessary part of the business model. You can't sell something that's publicly available. Exclusion of impoverished people—disproportionately Black and Brown—is not an unfortunate happenstance to be fixed but rather an intentional and critical part of the commodification of access to the workforce. The obstruction of some people's entrance into the workforce generates wealth for others.

Ours is quite far from being a free society. National studies show that Black and Latinx workers are overrepresented in low-paying high-risk jobs that are likely to be automated. Conversely, they are underrepresented in well-compensated, stable, and automation-resilient roles. White workers are about 50 percent more likely to hold those roles. Latinx workers face a 28 percent greater risk that their jobs will be automated than White workers do. Black workers face an 18 percent higher risk.[2]

Black and Latinx people are well aware of the ways they are shut out of certain roles. It's not that they are incapable of performing in those more stable jobs or are somehow less interested in them. It's not that entire races of people are making poor choices, as one would have to believe in order to endorse the narrative that ours is a free and just society. Indeed, one would need to believe in the supremacy of one race over all others in order to believe that we all have the same shot at prosperity. You would need to believe that the outperformance of White people in this regard is entirely earned and not indicative of any systemic advantage.

If entire groups of people can spend all of their time working and remain poor, their civilization has failed them.

A religious fanaticism has sprung up on the American Right around the word "freedom." It maps roughly to what the political theorist Isaiah Berlin refers to as "negative liberty," in his lecture *Two Concepts of Liberty*.[3] This refers to the absence of explicit constraints imposed by agencies of authority. I have the liberty to write this book on nights and weekends, because I don't have an employer making claims on that time. I have the liberty to devote my computer, my phone, and much of my coffee to the endeavor, because those things are mine. I bought them, and I can do with them whatever I want. I have freedom from restrictions in this domain, and so, within this domain, I am able to be my full self. Moreover, such moments of freedom, exercised by free people, work to advance a free society. Freedom *from* constraints is the basis of the American Right's interpretation of freedom.

However, their interpretation is incomplete. It's not enough to have freedom *from*. We must also have freedom *to*, which is Berlin's second concept of liberty, "positive liberty." If a manifestation of negative liberty is the absence of tyranny in the political sphere, positive liberty, by contrast, is the establishment of the democratic institutions necessary for citizens to exercise civic participation. We need more than just the absence of oppression; we need the resources to build its alternative. We need more than just freedom from a dictator. We need the freedom to elect the dictator's alternative.

Berlin's argument can be applied to economic freedom as well. We need more than the alleviation of poverty; we need the resources to build wealth. We need more than just the existence of good jobs; we need them to be attainable. We need more than a wage; we need to be able to realize a career trajectory through our strength of will. To be precluded from doing so by empowered people whose interests conflict with ours is a transgression against our positive liberty. It's a symptom of economic oppression.

Such is the case with the American working poor. As long as they have neither the time nor the resources to claim the freedom of upward mobility, they don't really have that freedom. They have negative liberty without positive liberty, which is to say that their liberty is incomplete.

The neoliberal use of the term "economic freedom," as coined by Milton Friedman, is similarly incomplete.[4] This idea, which forms part of the intellectual bedrock of a whole generation of conservative thought, is that a minimum-wage worker who is fed up with her job has the freedom, thanks to the law of supply and demand, to go get a better job. But does she, really?

She certainly has that negative liberty. She can quit without facing legal repercussions. But does she have positive liberty? Does she have the resources necessary to get that better job? If the better job requires a college degree, does she have the money for college? If the job requires expertise, does she have the free time to hone her skills or acquire the necessary new ones? Does she have the time to participate in the unpaid activities that could afford her some valuable experience, some references, and a few lines on her résumé? Does she have access to empowered people who will take a chance on her or connect her with others who will? Does she fit the profile that employers are looking for? She could be the most intelligent and hardest-working person in the world, but if she doesn't have the time, personal network, or capital, she does not have the freedom to walk out of that job.

For her to experience actual economic freedom, she must have access to the resources required to procure a better job. Her poverty has to be eliminated as a barrier to opportunity. The education necessary to upskill must be free, and the time needed for that education must be available. She might also need access to affordable childcare or the income necessary to keep the lights on, the house warm, and her family members' bellies full. Only once the conditions are met for this person to have the same opportunities as everyone else to acquire the skills necessary to live up to her potential can she be said to have the economic freedom to walk out of that job. Only then will the contours of her professional success be drawn by her own talent and work ethic and not by her current economic circumstances.

Tech is an opportunity if we can overcome tech culture.

In the struggle to develop viable pathways to prosperity, the tech industry represents a window of opportunity, for three specific reasons. First, the demand for tech jobs is high and resilient. According to the data in my Lightcast report, nearly a million job requisitions have been posted for software engineers nationally over the course of a year, persisting through the COVID pandemic. That's over quadruple the number of job requisitions posted for retail associates for the same period of time, when businesses were closed to the public. Retail has since made a huge comeback. Hiring rebounded in the months following the proliferation of the vaccines and the reopening of businesses in the spring and summer of 2021. But even through the height of post-COVID summer retail hiring, the number of job requisitions for software engineers remained about 30 percent higher than those for retail jobs. And that's just for software engineers specifically, a subset of the broader industry.

The tech boom will last. According to Lightcast data, demand in software engineering in the traditional labor market will grow by 30.7 percent over the course of the next decade. Projected growth in retail over the next decade, by comparison, is only 1.7 percent, as those jobs are highly vulnerable to automation. We're buying more and more of our stuff online. And when we do pop into a store, we're increasingly checking ourselves out at a kiosk. No one's bagging my toothpaste and shaving cream at CVS.

Second, tech jobs pay well, with salaries that start high and get higher quickly. The national average salary for a software engineer within the first two years of her career is currently about $83,900, according to my Lightcast report data. After just six to eight years on the job, the national average jumps up to $106,300.

At Resilient Coders, the cohort that graduated in December of 2020, during quarantine, saw an average starting salary of $92,400, despite the downturn. Before entering our program, these students had no prior coding experience, and few of them had bachelor's degrees. There's opportunity here, but the window won't stay open forever. The industry will experience a decline just like any other, and when it does, we'll pivot. But for now, there's a vein of gold beneath our feet. We may as well dig while it's there.

Third, the skills necessary to clinch tech jobs are at least *somewhat* objectively evaluated. Most nontechnical jobs require an evaluation of a candidate that is entirely subjective. Labor reports routinely bear this out. Topping every speculative list of the "skills of the future" is some variation of likability or pleasantness. Sometimes called "interpersonal" or "soft" skills, they represent the feelings of comfort and trust that the interviewer experiences while talking to the candidate. It's a measurement of a candidate's ability to satisfy the interviewer's cultural expectations. How well does this person stack up against my instincts around what the ideal candidate is supposed to be like? How is this person making me feel right now? Do they remind me of any successful people I know?

Unfortunately, what we call instincts cannot be disentangled from our deeply rooted racism, sexism, and phobias.

Technical careers afford us a chance for an objective evaluation. In theory, interviewers can get a sense of how well someone can code. When that happens, at least one aspect of an evaluation can be objective, as opposed to the standard interview, during which the entire evaluation is subject to the interviewer's instincts.

Standardized assessments continue to skew White and male. Even when they're gamified, as is popular in tech, and interviewers call them "challenges" and "scores" instead of using the term "standardized assessment," they're still standardized assessments. That said, an increasing number of companies are exploring alternate ways of determining a candidate's technical aptitudes. Some are experimenting with project-based evaluation. Others engage in pair programming, a practice in which two engineers—in this case, the interviewer and the candidate—build something collaboratively. None of this represents complete objectivity. But it's also not complete subjectivity. That's a step. But we have a long way to go.

Tech skills are also highly learnable. Too many of us grow up believing that software engineering, for example, is a career path reserved for geniuses. That's not true. Anyone can learn to code if they put in the work. Resilient Coders does not test applicants for aptitude when they apply to the program, nor have we ever dropped anyone because of aptitude. And yet, most of them get the jobs and keep them. Coding is a trade like any other. It's a discipline that can be learned, like any other. And anyone who says otherwise is trying to maintain scarcity in the talent pool and his dominance within it.

The minimum-wage worker who decides to follow Milton Friedman's advice and leave her job to pursue a career in tech will face at least two categories of barriers: She will need the skills to be a competitive candidate for the job. And, because our culture is predicated on exclusion, she will need to compete on a field rife with discrimination that invites certain people into tech and keeps certain others out. Those of us who work for skills training providers know this. We live with the uncomfortable truth that the work we do is not enough. Skills are not enough. There are systemic barriers that preclude entire communities of people from entering the workforce at a level that is commensurate with those same skills.

We need to give people the technical competencies that they'll need on the job. And we also need to completely transform tech culture. Neither of these efforts will ever be successful without the other.

Workforce development as an act of economic liberation

The field of workforce development was born out of crisis. The Works Progress Administration (WPA) was created by Franklin Roosevelt in 1935 in the throes of the Great Depression, as part of the New Deal, for the purpose of creating jobs for the unemployed. The people who took those jobs hadn't gone to college to study the history or technical nuances of their new jobs. They would need to be trained, but training was an investment that would yield abundant returns. Their employment would be a boon for them and their families, and it would spur the economic activity that the country needed at that time. And the labor performed by these workers was itself advancing public infrastructure, conservation efforts, and the arts.

This crisis hasn't ended, but it's changed. Workforce development remains a response to a humanitarian and economic need to train prospective workers, though for different jobs, in a different economy, and in a vastly different cultural and political climate. Today's programs are seldom training people to work directly for the federal government, as was the case under the WPA. Today, participating employers are typically private entities.

The process of training workers for private entities has introduced tension to the field of workforce development. The WPA was worker-oriented. Their objective was to employ the greatest number of people possible. What those workers actually did, the pace at which they did it, and the effectiveness with which they produced relative to time and capital were all less important than the primary objective of providing a reliable source of income. Workforce development programs today are, by contrast, employer-oriented. Even the most progressive private company is bound by commercial objectives that they need to achieve in order to stay in business. What the workers actually do and the efficiency with which they do it are more important than providing workers with stable well-paying jobs.

Private employers want to mitigate perceived risks, and so they minimize the investment in a prospective worker as much as possible, try to guess the likelihood of a candidate's success in advance of their employment, and closely surveil the worker's progress once they've started the job. This all makes sense in the context of protecting the employer's ability to perform against their commercial objectives. The desire to mitigate risk is rational. But it's hard to disentangle perceived risk from racist or sexist expectations. The hiring manager's rational inclination to hire more of the same people who've already been getting the job done validates her visceral preference for surrounding herself with her own people. The feedback loop of instinct and data is a hard one to disrupt.

At its best, contemporary workforce development is a diverse community of organizations committed to offering a countercurrent vision of access to jobs, a vision that is more consistent with that of a free society, in which the procurement of employment is not a reflection of class and privilege but of will and ability. The field is composed of a broad array of government entities, mission-based organizations, corporations, universities, public-private partnerships, and others, all offering a mosaic of services that collectively connect people to jobs. There are those that provide direct training and others that provide the support services that many of us require in order to be able to focus on our studies. Support services are especially important for the abatement of the symptoms of poverty; you can't study if you don't have food, shelter, stability at home, and stability within.

Workforce development is an industry in which the commercial needs of the paying client—the employer—are systemically misaligned with the purpose of the work. The employer wants an expedient and economically prudent talent pipeline. The workforce development community wants to provide the robust suite of services necessary to adequately support its constituents. The employer is going to center the needs of the employer. The workforce organization is going to champion those of the worker. Insofar as the field exists for the purpose of building alternative pathways to employment, they are alternative to the pathways preferred by their own partners, on whom they depend. It's a balancing act: The organization that advocates for too much on behalf of its constituents risks losing employers, thereby betraying the needs of its constituents. The organization that advocates for too little risks condoning substandard working conditions, thereby betraying the needs of their constituents.

The safe option for workforce development organizations is to stay in the good graces of those corporate clients. Each of us is aware that behind us in line is a host of other workforce development organizations and training providers that are comfortable acquiescing to the preferences of corporate partners. We have no common purpose across the field, which means we have no industry standards, which means we have no basic prerogative of unity. We're divided and in constant competition with one another, which makes any one of us easily replaceable to a client shopping for favorable terms. Without a clear expression of purpose and a popular commitment to its manifestation, workforce development is a capitalist enterprise like any other. It's the business of preparing some people to be assets to paying clients, in the manner and to the extent dictated by those clients.

Rather than simply focusing on procuring jobs, workforce development must unite around a shared aspiration to practice economic liberation. Moving toward this goal begins with unabashedly centering workers and alleviating the symptoms of poverty, so that people have an opportunity to shift their focus from surviving to thriving. Workforce development that centers its constituents offers skills training that is immediately relevant to the talent needs of industry and provides pathways to jobs that sustain families. No more settling for jobs with low wages and careers with low ceilings simply because employers pressure us to do so.

Liberation is bigger than skills training, so we must not stop there. Jobs cannot be the point of what we do but rather the vehicle by which we approach a much bigger objective: the recalibration of power in the workforce. This recalibration requires more than depositing workers into new environs and hoping that their technical skills are enough to vault them over the hurdles that we have chosen to ignore. We cannot continue to focus on the success of many persons while losing sight of entire peoples. We must be intentional about surmounting the obstacles that stand in the way of advancement. Somehow, while we vault over them, we must also dismantle them.

Part of this process requires the development of parallel institutions. It's not enough to create new points of entry into establishment institutions like college, because those new points of entry, like the old ones, will be dependent on the benevolence of their gatekeepers. In his book *The Power in the Room*, Jay M. Gillen describes "youth-determined educational and economic structures" that are parallel to young students' schools and traditional jobs.[5] The Algebra Project, the organization on which the book focuses, has a peer-to-peer knowledge-sharing network for middle and high school students that performs completely different educational functions from those experienced at a traditional school. The power structures are different. Relationships between mentor and mentee are different. The Algebra Project is not an addendum to school or a "support" program. It's a separate structure in which education is a dialogical act of exploration rather than a one-way depositing of information. One model foments and rewards critical thinking, the other compliance and rote memorization. The actual mathematical concepts being discussed between two young people might not matter that much in the long term. What matters is their discovery that parallel educational structures are possible, accessible, and bigger than the classroom. Gillen's description of the Algebra Project illustrates that when enough people with a shared vision realize they have power, cultures shift.

The Algebra Project is part of a broader movement to recognize the intersections between education, employment, and civic organizing. "Doing math looks like the typical occupation of the typical American adolescent," writes Gillen, "but while they do math, the young people are also learning how to resist the debilitating lessons of oppression and how to create and possess their own culture, their own representations and representative acts, their world."[6]

Once you realize that education can be a mutual act among peers and native to your community rather than a series of evaluations by a foreign power structure that operates independently of your community, you begin to see possibilities everywhere. You see opportunities for economic structures that are similarly liberated. You see political organizations differently. You realize that these are all social constructs, all of which depend on popular consent. All of these structures are made from the same bricks, and those bricks are all shaped from the same clay. There are no firewalls between educational, economic, and political liberation except the ones we've built ourselves.

This idea is revolutionary, but it's not new. In fact, it's at least hundreds of years old, persisting predominantly in Black and Indigenous political and educational resistance movements. The Algebra Project and other organizations like it don't exist for the purpose of mending the vulnerabilities of more "traditional" educational structures. They're building up parallel structures, from completely different roots, with different objectives. There's a big difference: At scale, they don't make our current educational system work better. They replace it.

The Algebra Project is not alone in this work. The United Teen Equality Center (UTEC), a youth workforce development agency that serves the cities of Lowell, Lawrence, and Haverhill, Massachusetts, is another great example of creating parallel structures. Their mission is "to ignite and nurture the ambition of our most disconnected young people to trade violence and poverty for social and economic success."[7] They run enterprises, such as woodworking and food services, that provide an income for the young people they work with, as well as training in skills that will carry over into future jobs. They offer "transitional coaching," which includes connecting their constituents to any additional resources they might need to be successful. They're active in the disruption of street violence as well, working with proven-risk and gang-involved young people, facilitating peace between gangs, and providing support to the court-involved. At UTEC, as at the Algebra Project, there are no firewalls between educational, economic, and political efforts. And those efforts are grounded in community, drawing strength and legitimacy from it, rather than attempting to operate independently of it.

It's important to contextualize the backdrop against which organizations like UTEC and the Algebra Project stand out. Because there's a propensity in the field of workforce development to adopt an employer-centric lens, some practitioners feel that employment services have the power and the responsibility to "fix" or "correct" people. Organizations like UTEC and the Algebra Project take the opposite approach, centering their constituents. They know that people have the power to correct the inhumane and discriminatory conditions of institutions.

While people are operating within oppressive structures and suffering the effects of that oppression, upskilling alone will never be enough. At some point we need to address the underlying causes of the symptoms we're treating. UTEC does this admirably. Significantly, their programs are all youth-led. They run social justice workshops. They're active in local and state politics, hosting youth-led fora with candidates for elected office. And they get young adults involved in statewide policy and advocacy work, developing their own legislative campaigns and agitating for their implementation. They recently led a campaign to amend state legislation around the expungement of youth criminal records.

UTEC and the Algebra Project have built parallel structures to those that routinely guide teen experiences. Similarly, Resilient

Coders is part of a community of organizations building pathways that are parallel to attending college. We're not interested in amending established institutions or broadening access to them but rather creating something that offers agency to our constituents, away from establishment gatekeepers. As a whole, we've been moderately successful in offering a viable and replicable alternative to the college-to-career track. We're relatively good, or at least comfortable, within that specific lane. Where our ecosystem has failed is one step further downstream. We have yet to build a viable alternative to the tech industry. When our students reach the end of our parallel structure, there is nowhere to send them but into the established industry. We haven't eliminated the need for our constituents to perform cultural contortions; we've only delayed it.

There may come a time when the work of building parallel structures extends into the tech industry. There's a rich tradition in Black American history of the development, out of necessity, of parallel economic structures, such as church-led "beneficial societies" (essentially early mutual funds), cooperative stores that allowed for the boycott of plantation produce, and a host of other community-based efforts that served to diminish their reliance on White vendors, customers, and employers.[8] It's reasonable to expect that similar efforts could develop in tech, given the fulfillment of three important conditions. First, more startups led by Black and Latinx entrepreneurs would need to be adequately funded. Crunchbase, a popular source of tech news, reports that even after a dramatic *quadrupling* of venture capital invested specifically in Black-led startups in the first half of 2021, that amount still only represents a miniscule 1.2 percent of the total $147 billion pie.[9] For context, Black people make up 13 percent of the population of the United States. That first obstacle can be overcome with money.

Second, the pool of trained talent from Black and Latinx communities would have to grow as well, such that entrepreneurs looking to staff their companies with people of color are able to do so. That problem, too, can be solved with money.

Third, consumers would need to want a parallel tech industry enough to favor it over the traditional industry. Enough of them would need to subscribe to the vision of a parallel tech industry to buttress it or to insulate it against a host of bigger and better-funded competitors from around the world. We've seen such support before, such as the use of niche social media platforms like MiGente and BlackPlanet. The question is whether or not the demand for a parallel tech community is big enough to employ a significant proportion of Black and Latinx people, and whether or not it's important to a significant proportion of Black and Latinx people to work in such a community. It's plausible, but it doesn't seem likely.

As long as we don't yet have the parallel economic structures necessary to employ everyone for whom working in a White-dominant corporate environment represents a shift in cultural norms, we need to be able to do two things: First, we need to materially transform tech culture, in order to make those spaces inhabitable for people of color. And second, while we work to transform those spaces, we also need to prepare people for jobs, right now, because rent's due at the end of the month. We cannot engage in movement building at the expense of the immediate needs of people.

Organizations like UTEC and the Algebra Project represent a specific type of intervention at a specific moment in a person's life. Not all organizations fit that particular profile, nor should they. As is the case in any industry, there's a robust network of workforce development organizations of all sizes, performing all sorts of functions in a variety of ways to serve their particular target audiences. In a healthy workforce development community, organizations collaborate, and there exists a system of pathways, with multiple onramps and offramps, across organizations, skills, and trades. A student might graduate from one program into another. A young person might work at Café UTEC during high school before enrolling in Resilient Coders and then choose to continue checking in with a member of the UTEC community throughout the program. We all want this person to be successful, so we pool our efforts and our resources toward the shared goal of eliminating the barriers inhibiting her ability to focus on herself and her journey.

The obstacles that come up for our students are predictable. They are symptoms of economic oppression. Those of us whose job it is to be there for our students show up and play whatever roles we can to enable their success. We've been to immigration court. We've raised money for legal fees and posted bail. We've gone shopping with students who don't have "professional" clothes. We've gone together to homeless shelters, to Alcoholics Anonymous meetings, to the weekly bilingual workshops that Vida Urbana runs in a church basement on how to protect oneself from predatory landlords. We're buying medications that aren't covered by public insurance. All of our efforts, within and across organizations, are not nearly enough, because the problems are the size of an entire economic system.

Much effort is spent duct taping together some form of temporary or one-time fix to problems that will continue to come up because they are the necessary and inevitable result of the system in which we all operate. We raised money for the family of an alum who was being deported by ICE after having committed no crime. That money may have bought some groceries, but that man should not have been arrested. We intervened in our small way, but the injustice persists. As you read this, more people are being corralled by ICE. We can't raise money for all of them.

Much of the work done under the banner of workforce development is not systemic but, rather, anti-systemic. They're individual acts of humanity. When systemic injustices challenge, minimize, or marginalize a person's humanity, personal acts that affirm that humanity are acts of resistance. This work is important enough that there should be professionals dedicated to it fulltime. Beneficiaries of these services deserve no less. They should be able to count on predictable, reliable, professional support.

This brings us to one of the paradoxes inherent in workforce development.

Poverty alleviation is a business.

Suppose, for the sake of a thought exercise, that we have all been, collectively, completely successful in our efforts to democratize access to the workforce. We have managed to forge a new, more just society, in which personal attributes or identities are no longer predictors of our professional success. Everyone has an equal shot at prosperity. Within the workforce development ecosystem, the sizable segment focused on achieving justice no longer needs to exist. By virtue of having achieved their goal, they have put themselves out of work.

This hasn't happened yet. In a sense, our collective failure to achieve our goal keeps us employed. The first paradox of workforce development is the fact that we draw our salaries because poverty persists. To be reductive for the sake of illustration: We're paid to alleviate poverty, and we continue to be paid because we've so far been unable to alleviate poverty. Unlike most fields, the degree to which we're successful is the measure of how much the industry can *shrink*.

There's nothing inherently wrong with the fact that people are paid to do this work. If we weren't being paid, the work would be done by volunteers, if at all. When roles are unpaid, those spaces fill up with people who enjoy the privilege of free time, jeopardizing any authentic connection between those leading and those being led. It's not uncommon for volunteer-powered work to descend into White Savior tropes, rife with the power dynamics of privileged White folx calling the shots, at the expense of the autonomies of impoverished communities. For workforce development to genuinely center the autonomies of the communities served, it must be led from within those communities; that's what autonomy means. The hours are long in this field, and broad impact is gradual. For the work to be sustainable longterm for people who do not have the privilege of substantial free time, it must be paid.

So who pays for this work, and why? Do they exert their influence on the nature of the work being done? Is there a catch? Money is not exchanged by accident; there's always a reason for a person or institution to spend, give, or invest. Even when it comes to charitable acts, in which the investor's expectation of return is different from that of a traditional investor or consumer, there are still returns. Donors may be interested in promoting a specific mission or advancing a cause that's personally important to them. They may donate in tribute to someone they love; as an expression of frustration over an injustice; as an act of solidarity; as a manifestation of values. It's a modest token of self-deprivation for the wellness of others. It's good for the soul. Donating can be prayerful.

Individual donors are not the only sources of revenue for workforce development. There are government funds. There are corporate social responsibility programs and family foundations. Student-funded and employer-funded models are popular. Most workforce development organizations depend on some combination of these sources of revenue.

Whether implicit or explicit, conscious or unconscious, the expenditure of money is powerful. Acts of power are acts of control, even when control is not the intention. An organization's biggest font of revenue is going to have some degree of influence. Whether this is a donor, a consumer segment, a government agency, or an enterprise client, the funded organization will want to keep that revenue. Conversely, one of the greatest positions of power and control that an organization can assume is that of not needing the money.

In order to understand workforce development and the relationships of power that develop within and around it, we need to ask some questions: Who is it that's funding this work, and why? Are the funding mechanisms democratic? To what degree, and in what ways, does funding influence the nature of the field?

At Resilient Coders, April 2020 was supposed to end with our Demo Day, the event at which our students present themselves and their work to a roomful of prospective employers. Typically at Demo Day, students speak for one minute each and then walk over to their respective stations throughout the space, where they open their laptops and present their work to interested employers. It is a reverse career fair, in a sense, with recruiters walking from station to station to meet candidates.

But less than a month into the COVID-19 quarantine and about two weeks before Demo Day, our companies began withdrawing. The economic impact of the pandemic had begun. Our employers had instituted hiring freezes and were predicting layoffs. We were facing the prospect of defaulting on our commitment to our students: you give us your best, every day, and we will put you in front of employers who want to hire you.

Our first priority has always been the continued physical, emotional, and financial wellness of our students. We needed to buy some time before dropping them from our payroll and releasing them into the worst labor market since that of their great-grandparents. We needed to extend our stipends.

A dedicated ally stepped forward, committing the money to keep all of our students paid for an additional ten weeks beyond their graduation date. There were no strings attached, no demands on how the program would be run. There was no presumption on his part, no dynamic of power, no glory. He asked to stay anonymous. With his gift, we established our Economic Resiliency Fund, which kept our students on our payroll. Additionally, we offered an advanced class to alumni who'd been laid off. The gambit worked. By the time the ten weeks had passed, we had been able to pull together a new coalition of employers. We ended the year with an 88 percent placement rate overall. The class that graduated in December 2020 saw our first-ever 100 percent placement. We never would have been able to do that without one generous person's intervention.

We're lucky. Our donors reflect the ideal profile: They trust us to make the best decisions for the organization. There's none of the sort of expectation of return with which other organizations have to contend. They give because they want to advance the work that we do and because they believe that our team is capacitated to do so. That takes a certain type of person.

Some of this is by design and by mutual selection. We tend to repel the wrong types of donors. People who expect their donations to "buy" them strategic authority over the way Resilient Coders operates don't donate.

Regardless, the relationships our community enjoys with our donors do not denote a system. To think systemically, we have to see beyond the wishes and intentions of individual people. We have to examine the role of the big donor within a broader landscape of power and recognize the influence they wield. Systemically, the small group of people who fund an effort like ours have influence. Something is purchased in any economic transaction. Whether it's in the context of a political campaign, an academic institution, a spiritual or religious one, or a nonprofit, big donors command the attention of leaders who are interested in sustainability and growth. As one donor put it, his donation "should have bought me a meeting with you." Transaction brings an expectation of influence. Zoom out to the ecosystem level: How comfortable are we with a system that serves the impoverished, who are disproportionately Black and Brown, being funded almost entirely by the wealthy, who are disproportionately White? Who has power here, really?

There is a counter argument: Big donations let us get back to work. From a purely operational standpoint, it's just more efficient to have fewer donors giving large amounts. It means more people working on the actual mission of the organization, and less on fundraising.

By contrast, grassroots fundraising strategies are more challenging. They require more time and more effort. If I want to raise a million dollars from a bloc of supporters averaging $50 per gift, I need to find twenty thousand supporters. Let's suppose for the sake of simplicity that, beyond our personal networks, we have a 5 percent conversion rate, from a person's first interaction with the campaign to the one-time donation of $50. To build the base of supporters needed to raise a million dollars, you'd need to engage with four hundred thousand people. This requires a press strategy, which costs money, and ads, which also cost money, and a sprawling fundraising team. The argument can be made in favor of a fundraising workforce that is predominantly unpaid, but this brings us back to the question of representation: Is the effort being run largely by those with the privilege of free time on behalf of those without it?

The overhead costs mean that a million dollars raised from small gifts is not a million dollars spent on the advancement of the mission. This is one reason leaders of fundraising organizations might prefer a strategy that is at least partially reliant on big donations. If I can walk out of a single meeting with a million dollars, then all the money I would have spent on my grassroots campaign can be spent furthering the actual work my team and I have set out to do. In April 2020, after my call with a donor, my teammates and I were able to devote all of our time to the wellness of our students and to rebuilding a coalition of employers. We spent no money on ads to attract small donations. It's no wonder that big donors are as sought-after as they are.

That said, there is a tradeoff to funding workforce development largely through big donors. It's the second paradox of workforce development, specifically in the nonprofit segment: The industry that exists for the sole purpose of ameliorating the harmful effects of unfettered capitalism works at the discretion of those who most benefit from unfettered capitalism.

Will using these donations to build parallel economic structures lead to a systemic overhaul? Probably not. Will the wealthy, as an entire class of people, contribute to building a future in which their kids don't have a disproportionate advantage over other people's kids? It seems unlikely. Will they champion organizations that intend to disrupt opportunity hoarding? Not many of them. I have met some incredible people who do. But that's no system. They're the exceptions, representing one more instance in which the most important work is done *against* the grain rather than with it. Their actions run countercurrent to the overwhelming tide of people who work to ensure their own continued enrichment. Those outliers are radicals. They are crucial, and they are too few. Having a few outliers does not constitute a systemic solution.

Some people think that a systemic solution is any effort that serves a lot of people. But this interpretation sidesteps the question of who actually has agency. It's the difference between delivering meals and creating the circumstances by which the people receiving the meals can buy or grow their own food. We have to do both, at the same time.

Arguably the most significant way in which philanthropy influences the direction of the nonprofit workforce development field is in the act of selection. They pick the winners. This influence isn't intrinsically positive or negative; that's not the point. The point is that their influence is immense.

Here's an example of how this plays out: Many wealthy families route their charitable giving through family foundations or trusts. These family foundations typically run a grant application process, and nonprofit organizations make a case for why they can make the best use of the family's money. Grant applications are reviewed, often by foundation staff, sometimes by a board of trustees, or by some combination of the two. Reviewers examine the contents of the applications against a rubric that is wholly their own. What they're looking for in a grant application differs from one foundation to the next, based on the foundation's strategic priorities and how an applicant organization's model, leadership, or outcomes make it "better" than the others. For example, some foundations are most interested in the breadth of impact, as determined by the number of people served. They might award a grant to an organization that runs a training program for ten thousand disenfranchised workers, though the depth of the proposed intervention may be minimal. Others prefer depth of impact per person, though fewer people are served. Neither approach is inherently right or wrong, so much as it is a reflection of their strategic priorities.

Some foundations believe it's possible to fight the harmful effects of capitalism with more capitalism. These foundations prefer workforce development organizations that elevate the employer's priorities or require students to pay for their education.

Employers want to save money on payroll; there are nonprofits ready to offer up a workforce that will work for less money. Employers often assume that people coming from "nontraditional" backgrounds are less capable than college graduates; there are nonprofits that allow these companies to pay their alumni less than they pay college graduates doing the same job. Employers want assurances that they're hiring "top talent"; there are nonprofits ready to administer standardized tests to applicants *before they join the training program*, though standardized tests skew White and male. Employers hesitate to make commitments to workers coming through training programs; there are nonprofits that are content with placement into internships that don't lead to full-time work. When employers say, "Jump," there's an entire community of nonprofits that ask, "How high?" And standing behind them is an entire community of capitalistic foundations with tape measures.

However these capitalistic foundations measure the magnitude of impact, they'll want to have achieved it as "efficiently" as possible, which is to say they want the greatest impact possible, achieved with the smallest amount of money. This comes at the expense of adequate salaries for nonprofit staff, the proportion of case managers to those who benefit from their services, "ancillary" services that are crucial for the abatement of symptoms of poverty, and stipends. This approach incentivizes a "race to the bottom" in which competing nonprofit organizations hack away at their own budgets in order to remain attractive to foundations, at the expense of their constituents. You might not technically *need* stipends in order to achieve your outcomes. You don't *need* that many social workers, if you can get fewer of them to take on more work and longer hours that eat into their evenings a bit.

The pursuit of impact as a commodity also lends itself to a commodification of trauma. If "impact" is understood by a nonprofit as the difference between a student's condition before and after the program, then the demonstration of impact in a grant proposal requires them to communicate what that initial condition was. It's one thing to place a college graduate in a job. It's harder to place someone without a college degree in that same job. Harder still if this person is impoverished, non-White, neurodivergent, trans or gender queer, or associated with any one of a host of potentially marginalizing factors or attributes. Some organizations are trying to clear more hurdles than others. In the nonprofit workforce development field, it's important that programs trying to clear fewer hurdles—suppose they place White college graduates into jobs—not detract financially from those working with more hurdles. But it's easy for this model to descend into a tendency to sell people's trauma for money to fund a program. There's a slippery slope when we compete to see whose trauma is more severe and who is somehow more deserving of training for a job.

In his *New York Times* opinion piece, "When I Applied to College, I Didn't Want to 'Sell My Pain,'" high school senior Elijah Megginson describes how he was encouraged to commodify his trauma in college applications:

> Each draft I wrote had a different topic. The first was about growing up without my dad being involved, the second was about the many times my life was violently threatened, the third was about coping with anxiety and PTSD, and the rest followed the same theme.
>
> Every time I wrote, and then discarded and then redrafted, I didn't feel good. It felt as if I were trying to gain pity. I knew what I went through was tough and to overcome those challenges was remarkable, but was that all I had to offer?[10]

This power dynamic, in which an empowered group of people are tasked with evaluating applicants based on whether their degree of trauma is sufficiently impressive, is deeply troubling. Megginson describes the effects that this act of mining for disadvantages has on the way his friends self-reflect. They begin to evaluate themselves according to their degree of disadvantage. Sometimes, they begin to see themselves as "less than" or "inferior." They can come to believe they somehow don't deserve to be present or to participate in certain spaces, such as expensive universities, compared to their classmates from more comfortable backgrounds. In the act of "selling" their disadvantage to the advantaged, they assume a perspective that positions their disadvantage as a defining characteristic. They're learning to see themselves through the eyes of a White-dominant power structure. They begin to worry that they may in fact be lagging behind their peers.

We see this dynamic play out all the time at Resilient Coders, from admissions to job acquisition and support. It's a common occurrence at our recruitment events that applicants appeal to our staff by emphasizing their disadvantages rather than their advantages. Many of our applicants come through the sorts of educational or nonprofit environments in which their pain has been collected and sold in bulk to philanthropic institutions. If you come up through the philanthropically funded nonprofit-industrial complex, in which you see that the kid selected to make the speeches at the galas is the one whose story is the one most rife with trauma, you can't help but learn that the empowered find value in your stories of trauma. You find yourself leading with your deficits rather than with your abundances.

The commodification of trauma is an important instrument in the neoliberal pursuit of efficiency in philanthropic giving. The argument is that the organization that can do the most with the least amount of money is the better one and therefore should be awarded more money in order to achieve exponentially more impact than the less efficient ones. But even without the exposition and evaluation of trauma, this argument requires a commodification of human beings. It means that when it becomes more expensive to serve Justin than Sam because of the symptoms of oppression to which Justin is more vulnerable, you choose to serve fewer Justins and more Sams. It means that when it's risky to set ambitious goals because doing so makes the program expensive, or because it jeopardizes your ability to post win after win in your annual report to donors, you start to move the goal posts a little closer. Your program begins to shrink as it accepts more students who are already closer to your vision of success, and you adjust your vision of success to be closer to where your students already are.

Systemically, two competing forces are acting on the nonprofit workforce development community: the impulse to do what's best for the organization is in conflict with the impulse to do what's best for the people it serves. It's sustainability versus humanity, and there is no shortage of nonprofit leaders lining up to offer the complement to the neoliberal business-first argument: The less-than-ideal program that can stay funded is ultimately better than a radically student-centric program that can't. Then you can best fight the system from within.

That's debatable.

Many foundations do get it right when awarding grant money. They evaluate breadth of impact without compromising depth or quality. They look for representation of the constituency served among the organization's leadership. They trust organizations to allocate their resources in a manner that is in the best interest of their constituents, rather than informing them how they must spend their money. They are interested less in charity than they are in justice. This ethos seems to have been gaining traction since the murder of George Floyd and the ensuing protests.

The common thread that runs across a diverse set of philanthropic institutions is the issue of representation. They make decisions that might deeply affect oppressed people, with no representatives of oppressed people among them or feedback from oppressed people. The flaw in this model is not necessarily the choices being made but rather who is empowered to make them. Trustees, philanthropy professionals, big donors, and nonprofit professionals are making decisions on behalf of others. Those decisions may affect the lives of those in the room somewhat, but they will most deeply affect the lives of those absent.

If we subscribe to Martin Hägglund's notion of freedom as the power to pursue self-actualization, then our freedom is measurable by the degree to which we have that power. The more power we have, the more control we have over our own destinies, and the more our personal and professional futures align with our hopes for them. Choice, power, and freedom are inextricably connected.

If we examine the influence of philanthropic foundations on the nonprofit workforce development industry, through the lens of choice as a proxy for power, we see that those with the most power are those who write the rules. Creating the rubric against which competing nonprofit organizations are evaluated is an act of power. Whoever creates the rubric determines what it is that matters most and searches for their values in others. One step down on the ladder are those foundation staff members who determine which organization best fits those values and executes them in a way that best fits the rubric. The nonprofit leader who can choose to accommodate her program such that it's most attractive to a foundation is exercising power, though less than the foundation, because she has less choice. The constituent who benefits from the nonprofit's services is empowered in that she can choose whether or not to participate. Her choice is binary. She has less power than the nonprofit professional, who has less power than the philanthropy professional, who has less power than the wealthy donors who have pledged their money. The industry that values efficiency in empowering the oppressed is not usually particularly efficient at empowering the oppressed.

Similarly, nonprofit workforce development is a democratizing force that is not particularly democratic.

As is the case with much of the nonprofit workforce development field, there are exceptions that run countercurrent to systemic tendencies. There are people in power who choose to forfeit or share their power. There are foundations that determine the allocations of funds by a popular vote among a diverse group of members who are not all big donors. There are nonprofit leaders who refuse to make program decisions purely in the interest of funding, and there are philanthropists who hear that refusal and pivot. There are nonprofit organizations within which constituents have real power. They might be represented in the organization's leadership team, or they might have spots on the board or on some other similarly vested council or body that has real authority over the strategic direction of the organization. But these examples are all exceptions. Power sharing remains a rebuke to, not a result of, the "natural" tendencies of the philanthropic system and the nonprofit industry.

CHAPTER 3

DISRUPTION OF SELF

A SCHOOL THAT MEETS its federal and state requirements is not the same as a school in which educators and administrators share a deep commitment to the work they do. Policy matters. Culture matters more. We can build lasting impact by shifting the tectonic plates of culture, even if that shift is completely unsupported by policy. The reverse is not true: policy unsupported by culture is tomorrow's backlash. It's a flimsy structure, ungrounded and vulnerable. It's cosmetic, when the real injury is internal. Conversely, lasting change, whether or not it's formalized into some sort of policy, is grounded in culture. Culture is based on our identities, the truths we share within those identities, and the narratives that both emerge from and reinforce those truths. Power is in the ideas we subscribe to collectively, the values we believe in, and the faith we have in those who exemplify those ideas and values. This is the nebula where the real power is.

Tech culture is fundamentally exclusionary, down to the way we interact with each other. We measure a person's worth by the cleverness (or "elegance") of a bit of code. We don't care about whether you solved the problem but only about *how* you solved it. When you talk about a project you worked on, we passive-aggressively enumerate the ways in which you could have done it a tiny bit better, in order to communicate that we are as smart as you are.

Do people in other industries do this? I wonder whether Miles Davis ever said to John Coltrane, "Hey that was pretty good, but technically if you used the trumpet, you'd only need one hand. I'm just saying, it's more efficient. Your way is good too though."

But tech culture is more than this. It's also in the books we read, the TED Talks we share, the heroes we celebrate, and the ethos we all bring with us to work. It's the lens through which we experience the world around us. Our concepts of what it means to build teams, collaborate, and push together toward shared objectives have turned us into hyper-productive industrial beasts of burden. Many techies are just now starting to look for *new* books, *new* TED Talks, and *new* heroes to help us recover our humanity, to bring us back to a sense of purpose that exists beyond the office. Particularly in the startup world, we've staked so much of our personal identities on this narrative of the headstrong pioneer who outworks and outsmarts everyone else that we've started to believe it. We really do think we earned the whole cake.

In 2015, Resilient Coders was selected to join a transformative startup accelerator called MassChallenge. An accelerator is essentially a bootcamp for young companies. About a hundred early-stage startups all worked together in a free shared office space, with access to amenities, knowledgeable mentors, services, and funding. We also had access to high-profile tech leaders, through various lectures and dialogues. At one such lecture, the founder of a major tech company conducted an exercise that I would later see replicated at other events. He pulled a twenty-dollar bill out of his wallet and held it out to the audience. "Who wants it?" he asked. We didn't really know how to respond at first. A few people raised their hands, but that didn't seem to be what the founder was looking for. A moment later, some people started shouting for it. That didn't work either. Eventually, a guy seated way in the back got up from his chair and started jogging up toward the stage. Another man, already seated in the front, turned and saw the guy jogging up from the back. He jumped out of his own chair, beat the other man to the stage, and snatched the twenty from the founder's hand. The guy who'd been jogging up from the back row went back to his seat.

"There it is," said the founder. "If you want it, you need to jump up and grab it!"

"That's not what I took from this lesson," said someone else from the back. "I think you've illustrated the fact that some people have better access to money than others, for reasons that have nothing to do with how much they want it."

They parried a bit. The founder limped through a losing argument before moving on with the rest of his lecture. I don't believe it had ever occurred to him before that moment that some people have better access to money than others. This man really believed that when he stood up from his own seat and achieved success with his company that he had been the most deserving of that success among a level playing field of equals, that he'd been the first, the smartest, and the hardest working, that he'd been the visionary.

We startup folx see ourselves as rebels. We're the unlikely heroes, the underdogs, punching ever upward, striking at the heart of the empire. We think of Steve Jobs, twenty-one years old and wearing an ill-fitting suit, having the audacity to suggest that the machine he built with a friend could end IBM's monopoly. Tech culture is ridiculous. It's also bold, inspiring, and, to some of us, intoxicating.

Our image of ourselves and our culture reflects a recurring trope of White-dominant American storytelling. We're Han Solo, making the Kessel Run in twelve parsecs. We're Luke Skywalker, the farmer with an attitude and a destiny, at the margins of the Empire. And as is the case with most cultures, our legends interact with our history, like two walls in the same echo chamber. The true stories from our national past intermingle with the fables with which we entertain and inspire each other, and this hybrid mythology reverberates, grows, and evolves with us. In our own minds, we're forever the ragtag shoeless American patriots. We have in our national cultural DNA traces of those farmers and tradesmen who, gripping their rifles, prepared for a surprise attack on the bigger, stronger, and more heavily armed mercenary forces across the river in New Jersey. "We cannot insure Success," wrote John Adams to his wife in 1776. "But We can deserve it."[1] The idea that we deserved that victory speaks to a core tenet of our national identity that has persisted for hundreds of years: we are capable of outworking, outsmarting, and outmaneuvering the greatest of empires. Such is the credo of the entrepreneur.

Of course, in doing so, we build new empires. The republic founded by those ragtag shoeless patriots would become a powerful empire with its own overseas colonies. The presence of these territories, in which the residents have no influence in the government that rules them, is largely absent from our national mythology. Tellingly, the Star Wars franchise managed to produce three trilogies in which the rebels consistently win and yet somehow never seem to assume power. They simply maintain a perpetual state of rebellion, with each trilogy featuring a new imperialistic presence to be overthrown. They avoid altogether the thorny issue of rebels becoming the new rulers. No one wants to watch a film about Empress Leia ruthlessly crushing dissent, because that would be a departure from our collective identity as perpetual rebels.

This is the bedrock on which tech startup culture rests. This is the self-image we affirm when we take a job with longer hours and less stability than a more traditional job. We seek out those jobs, or we create them, out of our spirit of entrepreneurship. Our motivations are not rational but visceral. Our choices are an expression of who we are. We're changemakers, pioneers, and visionaries. We're *disruptors.*

Ours is a culture that tends to deify the word *disruption,* as though it were an act of democratization or power recalibration. Uber has disrupted the sclerotic taxi industry and allowed anyone with a car to make money. Airbnb has disrupted the multibillion-dollar global hospitality industry and opened the door for countless homeowners to leverage their own properties on their own terms. And tech culture is not just about disrupting other industries. Calling your business a startup is also an unspoken commitment to an ethos of continued self-disruption. Savvy startups disrupt themselves. They study their own weaknesses. They keep themselves in a constant state of experimentation. If you have the humility to understand that your business will inevitably be disrupted, you focus your efforts on being the one to do it.

The winds have changed. It's time for a disruption of the culture of disruption. And since change is concentric, we start from within.

Our relationships with time and community

"We got it," I said, tapping the stopwatch on my phone. We were just shy of five minutes. It had been a goal of mine to be as efficient as possible with our meetings. There were five of us on my team at PayPal at the time. We'd each managed to report the prior day's activities and our goals for the rest of the day in less than a minute. This was in pursuit of efficiency for efficiency's sake, but I also regarded it as an expression of respect for the rest of my team. Time was our currency. It's finite. It's precious. And to demand it of others is a big ask. There are implications when you request a meeting: I as your manager have power over the way you spend your time, to whatever extent I want. Whatever else you're doing is less important than whatever I want you to do, in support of the goals *I* want to accomplish. My priorities matter more than your priorities.

In trying to demonstrate respect for my colleagues, I was squeezing our interactions into minute-long blocks of time. I wanted to listen to what the members of my team had to say, as long as they could keep it to the length of time it took me to unscrew the cap from my thermos, take a few sips of coffee, nod meaningfully to whatever they were saying, replace the lid, and set it back on my desk. After that, let's all get back to work.

A cornerstone of this style of management is the conviction that what people really want to be doing is producing for the company, not attending meetings. This may be true for a lot of us, including me. I loved the work I did at that job. But let's not forget that the purpose of the practice is to maximize efficiency in the production of commercial goods. The fact that many of us enjoy the individual craftwork we do when we're not in meetings is incidental and applies only to those who enjoy the privilege of doing what we love. "Do what you love" is a core tenet of startup culture. It's on the job descriptions; it's on the agendas of startup conferences; there are books on it and motivational speakers dedicated to it. If your startup is headquartered at one of WeWork's buildings, you've probably been drinking your coffee out of mugs with "do what you love" printed on them. Maybe you've even bought the shirt. A whole religion has sprung up around this slogan.

It follows that if you love what you do, you don't mind doing it all the time. We have normalized the weekend grind. We venerate the late-night Chinese takeout brainstorming session, in which four or five pioneers take over a conference room and cover it in Post-its, brightly lit against a dark city skyline. It's fun, if it only happens occasionally and you love what you do. It's especially fun if you enjoy the same music and watch the same movies as your colleagues and laugh at the same cultural references. It's a blast if you're roughly the same age and if everyone is okay with having a little beer onsite.

It's significantly less fun for the person who has to go home to take care of a child or go to a second job. She'll miss those moments with the team. Much of tech culture is predicated on homogeneity. This is largely because tech historically sourced its talent from similarly homogeneous environments like the computer science programs at expensive universities, which have in turn sourced their students from similarly homogenous high schools. Once you're already in such an environment, it's hard not to perpetuate it with every new hire. We like our own kind. We want to surround ourselves with people who get our references and who are so culturally proximate that relating is easy and comfortable. We want to hire those people who spent last weekend building an application that listens for the opening theme song of *Firefly* and automatically sends a request to our popcorn machines. It's our culture, celebrated in our way, with our humor, our tools, and the spare time we assume we all have. It was once common practice in the field, while evaluating a candidate for a job, to ask fellow interviewers whether the candidate was someone with whom we wouldn't mind being stuck at an airport. The point of the question, and others like it, was to try to avoid friction between this new recruit and the rest of the team. This is inextricable from cultural bias. I might not have much in common with a Chinese émigré my mother's age if we were stuck at an airport together. But she could be a powerful contribution to my engineering team.

In our relentless pursuit of efficiency, we begin to evaluate each other accordingly. Our relationships with each other and with our own selves rest on how much and how well we think we can produce. The cult of productivity has influenced our sense of value. This is the techie version of keeping up with the Joneses: Bill spent the weekend teaching himself this cool new programming language we read about on Hacker News while I was wasting my time sledding with my kid. In Bill's value system, which centers a productivity-oriented hierarchy, he is superior to me. Everyone on my team at work buys into this value system. Should I?

Do I choose to identify with a culture in which my worth as a person is predicated on how much of my life is spent in front of a screen? Or do I choose to live my life such as I want to live it and understand that my colleagues will see me as mediocre?

The cult of productivity is a big part of tech culture. Layer over that our bigoted instincts of who is and who is not most likely to be productive. The neurodivergent, the elders, the obese, and really anyone who appears to our eyes somehow unwell or unhealthy— do they seem like the candidates most likely to conform to our culture? What about the Black or Latinx, or the working class?

There's a difference between gatekeeping as a necessary part of the hiring process and gatekeeping as a culture that people defend with religious zeal. Just as there is a difference between being able to afford the house in the affluent neighborhood and feeling as though you belong in the affluent neighborhood.

Tech does have a counterculture. More and more tech workers are participating in movement-building efforts to shift tech culture toward a value system based on inclusion rather than exclusion, and this shift has accelerated since the murder of George Floyd and the subsequent uprisings. But these workers face a significant obstacle: They too are steeped in the culture that they seek to change. Most techies understand that they have a lot to learn. But most don't realize that they also have a lot to unlearn.

The cult of productivity in which we came up gets in the way of our efforts to remake ourselves as organizers. Our relationships are more often transactional than transformational, because that's what we know. That's what we're doing when we evaluate ourselves and each other on the basis of our industrial talents. Transformational relationships are something else entirely. They demand that you see your peers for their humanity and not their industrial output. Transformational leaders are those who are able to measure a person by her own scale. They don't have a single value system they impose on others but rather a plurality of value systems that they've gleaned from others. This is the opposite of what we've come to admire in tech leadership. You can't aspire on Monday to be the eccentric and misunderstood genius who cares more about his work than his relationships with small people and then on Tuesday turn yourself into Fannie Lou Hamer.

Our relationships with scale can also make us poor organizers of people. Scalable applications are scalable because they are lean. Scalable business models are scalable because time, talent, and capital are leveraged efficiently. Kill your meetings, get back on the keyboard.

Social structures in tech are designed for efficiency. One of the startup industry's great innovations has been the flattening of hierarchy. Compared to traditionally structured enterprises with multiple levels of managers, tech startups and the bigger companies that emulate them have fewer rungs separating the intern from the CEO. This gives the appearance of democratization. It also happens to be efficient. But a flattened hierarchy doesn't make a company a collective or a cooperative. Strategy is still set at the top. And while cells within the company may operate with a certain level of autonomy, they're still working within the bounds of a strategy that's been set at the top. They have the autonomy to choose how to execute against the goals that they've been handed.

This is a necessary structure for an innovative capitalist enterprise. Commercial success depends on efficiency, which requires alignment among staff toward a common goal. The problem is that techies, who spend their days participating in a top-down model of doing business, have a propensity to bring this approach to their organizing work. They establish top-down organizing models, which center efficiency and productivity. In such a system, everything that is inefficient or unproductive is anti-systemic. Listening to people before developing a strategy is inefficient. Allowing some people to function autonomously is inefficient. It is difficult, maybe impossible, for a hierarchically flat collective to develop a strategy that is comprehensive, effective, and bold.[2] That's not how good strategies are created. Good strategies must be based on the group's shared culture and values. Culture and values come from everyone. Those who aspire to participate in movement work need to enter every conversation with the expectation that they will learn something. This is antithetical to tech culture, where people enter into every conversation looking for an opportunity to teach.

Tech moves at the pace of tech. Humans move at the pace of humanity. And the organization of human beings scales from interactions that don't scale. It's not efficient. It's not about sprints. It's definitely not about strongly worded messages or emails. It's about investing in relationships and building trust with people over time. It's not through the power of ideas that we gain momentum but through the power of interpersonal trust and the million small things on which it rests. You might be a visionary, but if I don't trust you, it doesn't matter. If you're searching frantically for your coalition once you need it, you've already lost.

The strength of Resilient Coders is in the strength of our community. We invest in it in ways that don't scale. Our community-building is inefficient, messy, and untethered to any expectation of immediate output or "progress." Our community is composed of human beings whose selves are much bigger than their utility to us or to our mission. We care about each other, as humans. We show up for each other, as humans.

We break bread together. Before the pandemic, our managing director of engineering and his partner would open their home every Friday night to any alum or member of staff who wanted to drop by. It was our weekly Pasta Night. Cooking started at seven, but you could drop in whenever, with whomever. There was no agenda, no objective or "purpose" beyond gathering around the table. With the onset of the COVID lockdown, we pivoted. Alumni organized Friday night movie nights. They'd vote on a movie to watch simultaneously on Netflix, each in their own home. We had a book club, which began with a discussion of Assata Shakur's autobiography.

We've given authority to our alumni over which volunteers are, or are not, allowed in the classroom. We have an online community for healthy living, in which people organize bike rides and share recipes. There's another for artists interested in sharing their work. We have an active job board, as well as a help forum in which people ask each other technical questions. The communities are diverse in nature but similar in their spirit of mutual empowerment. There's no lecturing or unilateral depositing of information. We don't have experts coming in to lead workshops or webinars. No one "runs" any of these fora. Growth is collective.

The culture at Resilient Coders can feel like a departure to people whose notion of purpose is founded in their expertise. It's common for tech professionals to reach out to us, offering to lead workshops, universally already having selected their topics. That's understandable; we all know our domains. But when we tell them that their chosen topic is not particularly relevant to our curriculum, they balk. Their commitment to a self-image predicated on expertise cannot accommodate the idea that their topic may not be relevant to us. Nor can they abide the insinuation that our community may know what's best for our community. It becomes important to them that we be wrong, because they must be right, as a matter of fundamental truth.

Still, we're open to their presence in our community, if they approach as members rather than luminaries. But no one who's ever started their relationship with Resilient Coders with the intention of lecturing has ever stuck around. "It's not a good use of my time," said one. Another sent me external validations of their expertise as evidence that they belong in front of our students rather than next to them.

This is the attitude that precludes tech workers from organizing. What may be the most empowered workforce in the history of work cannot effectively organize because it doesn't prioritize the development of its communities. We have an appetite for differentiating ourselves from our peers, rather than elevating them, in our relentless pursuit of individual superiority.

In addition to the cultural barriers in tech that make organizing difficult, there are structural incompatibilities as well. The values we associate with the sort of community-building we want to do may not actually work within the context of business. There's a certain profile of a leftist techie who wants their company to be innovative, collectivist, and pluralist. But realistically, of those three, we can pick two. We can be innovative and collectivist, as long as we have uniformity of thought throughout the collective. We can be innovative and pluralist, as long as actual decision-making is concentrated in the hands of a few. And lastly, we can be collectivist and pluralist, as long as we're not also trying to be innovative. Innovation requires bold and often unpopular decision-making. Nothing kills innovation quite like having to arrive at consensus among a group of people with different objectives, perspectives, and priorities. That's the United States Congress, designed to be slow and reactive.

Our relationships with community and power

Cultures are built on common narratives and myths, and tech culture is no different. In an effort to substantiate our self-image as the perpetual rebel forces who've spent nine movies winning rebellions without ever assuming power, we've created a story for ourselves around power sharing. We've allowed ourselves to believe that tech is somehow more democratic or egalitarian than other industries. As is the case with any culture, we validate our self-image with folklore.

There's the "don't take outside money" parable. For years, the expectation for startup founders is that they take a good idea and a proof of concept to a cohort of venture capitalists, who then infuse the company with money, and the founders can then get to work bringing their good idea to life. This model is not just practical, it's also cultural. Raising money is a status symbol, like a musician getting signed to a record label. And just like musicians getting signed to labels, success can sometimes breed resentment over the loss of control. In recent years, some entrepreneurs have popularized the idea of holding off on accepting outside money, like musicians choosing to produce an album independently. In the immensely influential book *Rework*, serial entrepreneurs Jason Fried and David Heinemeier Hansson have a chapter called "Outside Money Is Plan Z."[3] The idea has continued to gain traction in startup folklore in the decade since the book's publication. And why wouldn't it? There's a certain romanticism to the idea of remaining wholly independent of outside influences, accountable only to oneself. An indie musician is free to explore their own artistic vision, unencumbered by the commercial demands of a major label. Few words are more resonant in America than "independent." And few words are more complicated.

Refusing to accept outside money is a very American expression of the word "independent." People who are already in positions of power eschew the authority of institutions they see as being in positions of even greater power. In this scenario, power is available for the taking, but only to those who already have it. In the startup ecosystem, money is influence. Investors might want a say in how the company's run. Startup founders who want to remain independent of the influence of investors will have to get their money somewhere else—often from friends and family. Mom and Dad don't need quarterly reports. But what about the founders who can't raise a million dollars from friends and family? Can they be "independent?" Or is "independence" only for the privileged?

Exclusion features prominently in tech folklore. The "pull yourself up by the bootstraps" myth lulls us into believing that our success in tech has been entirely earned. The "I'll hire the best person for the job" myth sounds progressive because it suggests that the speaker is indifferent to whether or not a candidate has a college degree. But every time we've heard that declaration at Resilient Coders, candidates have then been routed through recruitment processes that select for privilege and pedigree. They are presented with coding challenges that test for the skills learned in a computer science degree program but never actually used on the job. This is a bit like asking your car mechanic to explain the physics behind combustion before giving her the keys to your car. It's cool if she can do it, but I promise you, it does not make her a better mechanic. It just dramatically and needlessly shrinks your pool of mechanics to choose from.

We don't have to accept any of this folklore as reality. We can choose to be better. But it requires more than talking about it.

It's generally those who do the most talking that do the least doing. It's the well-intentioned ally who indulges in a violent tirade in an email to the whole company that alienates everybody and accomplishes nothing. It's the social justice warrior immobilized by unending navel-gazing. It's the person for whom social justice is a platform for self-expression and catharsis, and who is so focused on the struggle within that they have no bandwidth for the struggle without.

We like to blame companies for their inaction. But companies are just a gathering of individual people. When people who are mollified by talk enter into a community of other people who are also mollified by talk, you get a company that mollifies with talk. If your company's leadership makes statements but doesn't actually do anything, it's because statements are all that you and your colleagues require. Blaming a whole company for the inaction of people keeps us from understanding the real root of the problem. The CEO is a single token in a broader landscape of power.

We do a lot of mollifying in tech. In his *Boston Globe* article "'Nothing Actually Changes,'" reporter Pranshu Verma points out that "technology companies that made statements of solidarity with the Black community after the murder of George Floyd employed 20 percent fewer Black employees on average than those that didn't."[4] Statements have become a stand-in for action. We shouldn't be surprised. That's the price for which we've sold our satisfaction as workers. As long as talk is all we want, talk is all we'll get.

Solidarity is not spoken, it's exercised. And in the struggle for economic justice, tech is uniquely positioned to exercise it.

Too many Americans don't make enough money to live in their cities. Tech pays well.

Too many jobs on which our communities depend are under immediate threat of automation. Tech jobs will grow.

Too many people work jobs in which their performance is evaluated entirely subjectively. Their professional futures are, by design, subject to their colleagues' biases. Tech jobs afford a certain level of objectivity.

Other industries move only as far and as fast as their inertia will allow. Tech is the business of radical change. It's the arena in which new things get done. It's the industry of fast action, constant innovation, and iterative improvement. Technologists embrace failures as necessary steps in authentic experimentation. We've disabused ourselves of the idea that real progress is linear, and we know that the appearance of linear progress is either an act of theater, or it's an indication that the bets are too small. We solve problems, to the extent that we want to solve them, at the pace at which we want to solve them. And then we solve them again, a little bit better than the last time. We in tech need to make economic justice a problem that we want to solve. It *has* to be in tech, and it *has* to be now. Tech culture is due for disruption. And not just within the leadership. Culture comes from everyone.

CHAPTER 4

DISRUPTION OF INDUSTRY

THOSE OF US who provide skills training as a means to pursue economic justice live with an uncomfortable truth: It's not about the skills. Training alone will bring us no closer to justice. There are systemic obstacles precluding people of color from entering the workforce at a level that is commensurate with their skills, no matter how skilled they are. If skills training were the answer to racial wealth disparities, then people with comparable skills would earn comparable salaries, regardless of race. That's not the case.

The study *What We Get Wrong about Closing the Racial Wealth Gap* finds that educated White people and comparably educated Black people do not enjoy the same degree of wealth. In fact, the difference is quite stark: "At every level of educational attainment, the median wealth among black families is substantially lower than white families. *White households with a bachelor's degree or postgraduate education (such as with a Ph.D., MD, and JD) are more than three times as wealthy as black households with the same degree attainment.*"[1] On average, a White household whose head has no college degree *still* has more wealth than a Black family whose head has a college degree. Any solution to the wealth gap predicated solely on skills training is missing the point.

Ta-Nehisi Coates laid out these disparities during a 2016 appearance on *The Daily Show*, when he explained to host Trevor Noah, "If I have to jump six feet to get the same thing that you have to jump two feet for—that's how racism works."[2] For years I told our students that there's nothing Resilient Coders can do about that four-foot split but build a springboard. That's fundamentally what the bootcamp model is. We're a vehicle by which people of color can hurl themselves the necessary six feet up and over the wall that stands in the way of their professional success. We've gotten very good at this at Resilient Coders, maintaining high placement rates and high starting salaries. But in a way, we've gotten *too* good at this. We've normalized the springboard. We've attracted spectators, who clap and cheer when they should be horrified by the persistence of the wall. Our success has allowed people to believe that we represent a "fix to the system," as though the solution to the chronic inequality endemic to "the system" is to ask some people to just keep muscling through it, forever. As long as we see interventions like ours as viable long-term solutions, we're not ending inequality; we're aiding and abetting it.

We're tired of having to launch our graduates into the stratosphere to afford them a shot at the bottom rung of someone else's ladder. We've been springboarding for too long. It's time to confront the wall. And we need you with us.

I wrote this book for you, to pull you in, because you are needed. This book is meant to be direct, actionable, and ephemeral. It will expire, because it's a product of a particular moment beyond which we have to advance. This is not a book you save. It's not a book you "like," or "dislike," because your approval matters less to me than your sense of urgency. This is a book you read quickly and share.

There is a place for books that offer theory or idyllic systems of political or economic thought. That's not what this is. I'm not interested in being a theorist. This book is meant to be expedient, tangible, and consciously imperfect, since perfection is the enemy of progress.

Conscious imperfection for the sake of expediency has its roots in the Buddhist concept of *upaya*. This is a pathway to enlightenment that is not itself necessarily enlightened. Rather, a person says what needs to be said to reach a noble goal. The Lotus Sutra features a parable of a wealthy man in a burning house, promising elaborate carriages to his children if they leave quickly. He doesn't have the privilege of ideological purity. The house is on fire.

This is a book for the people smelling smoke.

Build

"Theory without practice," says Assata Shakur in her autobiography, *Assata*, "is as incomplete as practice without theory."[3] She is writing about the struggle for Black liberation in the 1970s, expressing her frustration with the intellectual performances she witnesses from some of the movement's leaders. Theory is important, but there's not an essay in the world that can put food into the mouths of the hungry. Theory must elicit practice. And theory must also emerge *from* practice. Each shapes the other.

Shakur is reacting to her experience in college, watching the members of student organizations deliver soaring speeches to other members of their same organizations, people who already agree with them. If the words won't move anyone, she asks, why speak them?

We're doing the same thing now when we perform on social media for people who already agree with us. Though truthfully, there's no difference between someone who agrees and someone who doesn't if neither will do anything about it. Their personal approval or disapproval doesn't matter. The leftist, the conservative, the radical, the centrist, the fundamentalist, the socialist, the ally, the advocate, the troll, the fascist, the capitalist, the Klansman, the artist, the optimist, the realist, the liberal, the libertarian, the feminist, and the moderate are all just people typing on their phones, entertaining themselves during the dead space between events in their day. Once their coffee order is up or their partner returns from the bathroom or the commercials end, they go on with their lives. And ultimately, nothing actually happens. As long as no one's actually done anything, the movement has moved neither forward nor backward.

This is also true with performative statements. Don't tell me you care. Care.

I don't believe what people say. I believe what they do. It's especially true when discussing the efficacy of those who call themselves activists by virtue of the things they say. These are the people whose ideals are unfettered by reality. They value ideological purity above all else; they won't bother with the tedium of community service, nor with the complicated work of advocating for real people with real needs, nor even in really listening to them. You don't build much without getting your hands dirty. Building is messy. But for some, it's not about building so much as it is about personal gratification, personal identity, and personal validation. That's theory without practice, and it just stays within your person.

I often get what people call "attacks from the Left," but I don't see anybody out here on the field. They must be so far to the left they're in the bleachers, totally removed from the game and enjoying their popcorn as they watch. You can recognize a real leftist by the sweat on their brow, not by the platitudes they say they stand for.

Ideological purity leads to immobilization in those who might have otherwise been fighters. They want to participate, but they don't want to get it wrong. They're afraid to overstep or stray, because the blowback from the purists can be brutal. They don't want to speak, because they might say the wrong thing or say the right thing the wrong way. They don't want to act, because the blowback could wake them up from the warm buzz of absolute conviction. And what if they're judged? What if they're resented?

I get it. But this is how we lose good people, and right now we need them on the field. We can't afford to lose people to the fear that they might do something wrong, because doing something wrong is inherent in experimentation. And without experimentation there is no actual progress. Go out and get it wrong, so that you can eventually get it right.

Start failing at things. Be bad at stuff. Whatever you choose to do in pursuit of economic justice, such as overhauling your recruitment efforts or launching an internal on-the-job training program, normalize the fact that you will get it wrong the first time. Lean into the discomfort of letting people down; discomfort is your greatest teacher. Enter into every conversation, with everyone, with the expectation that you may learn something. If you do, you will. Develop a relationship with your own failure. Understand how you react to it. Accept it. Consume the lessons that come from it, and then throw away the packaging. You may not be good at throwing away the packaging right away, and that's all right. You can start by giving yourself permission to try. Show yourself a little grace.

Progress requires experimentation; experimentation requires failure. Normalizing failure requires resilience, and resilience in its purest form is wellness and self-love.

I've had to disabuse myself of the idea that resilience is about self-deprivation. It's true that the path towards your own greatness might be occasionally punctuated with sleepless nights and tightened belts. That's often the reality. But you also need to invest in your own longevity. Resilient people can survive a drought because they've kept the well full; there is no evolved species that needs no water.

This work is emotionally exhausting. You need to invest in your self-love. It's your wellness that feeds your resilience; it's your resilience that grants you the grace to fail and try again the next day. It's your ability to fail that allows you to experiment, and it's experimentation that eventually yields progress.

As you advocate for others, don't forget to advocate for yourself. This is hard. At some point, you'll find yourself feeling guilty prioritizing your wellness over your work. Your wellness matters in its own right, but if it's important to you to frame it as such, know that your wellness is also important to the sustainability of your struggle and to those who depend on you. When you forestall your personal completeness until you're "done" with your struggle, whatever that might mean to you, you will be forever looking for a conclusion to your work so that you can rest. A fighter who can remain complete throughout the fight can fight forever. Learn to remain complete while you fight. We need you to stay in it.

You will forever undermine your own resilience as long as you require validation from other people. Understand what you can and cannot control—and most things are beyond your control. Other people's reactions to you are beyond your control. What you do is within your control. If you know that whatever controversial step you took was the right thing to do, take refuge in that knowledge. Find peace in it. If you messed up, own your failure. Accept it. Lean into discomfort, your greatest teacher. Learn from it. And then move on. We need you to find a way to move on.

Conduct a personal audit of your sources of strength, and then invest in them. Write them down, if you need to. Nourish them, through moments of hardship as well as those of relative peace. They're like friends: If you only ever call on them in times of need, they may come through, but you will eventually exhaust them. Strengthen that which strengthens you, during both war and peace.

No service without action. No action without service.

Just as theory and practice complete each other, so do political action and service. They're two sides of the same coin. They mutually support, advance, and define each other. Protest without service is just talk. Service without protest is charity, and the entire construct of charity is incompatible with justice. Service without protest is better than no service, but it won't lead to systemic change. Opening another homeless shelter is important for the dignity of those who benefit from it, but it won't cause us to examine the systemic injustices that have caused the shelter to become necessary. Service *with* protest is resistance.

Service for the actualization of an agenda of liberation offers an alternative to an unacceptable status quo. It's a rebuke to the idea that "well, this is just how it is." Resilient Coders doesn't train people for engineering jobs because we feel bad that some people don't have access to expensive colleges. We're not here to patch up the leaks in a model to which we otherwise subscribe. We're here to challenge that model. We connect people with engineering jobs as a way of demonstrating that we don't need those expensive colleges. We *shouldn't* need them, and we *don't* need them. Every alum is a case in point. With every raise and every promotion, our whole community takes a step forward. The advancement of people is also the advancement of a broader agenda. An alternative reality is possible, and better. We represent a parallel structure to our society's deeply classist and racialized paths to prosperity.

Parallel structures are constructed as part of a broader resistance program. The mujahadeen built schools as part of their resistance against Soviet occupation. Gandhi famously spun his own clothes, celebrating traditional Indian culture while also boycotting the exploitative British textile industry. We have a rich tradition in our own country of building parallel economic structures to boycott or resist an exploitative "mainstream" industry. With just about any purchase you make, from eggs and bacon to your retirement account, you have the option of buying an alternative version that's supposed to be more ecologically, ethically, or socially responsible (though, as always, the truth is a bit more complicated than the marketing). The meatless industry is fundamentally a parallel economic structure. It functions as part of a broader resistance agenda.

Parallel economic structures don't exist in isolation. They serve a bigger picture. The meatless industry is a window into an alternate reality without factory farms. It's an artifact of a civilization in which people's values are incompatible with the routine exploitation of animals, laborers, and the planet. It's tangible evidence that a better society is possible.

Imagine a parallel society in which Black and White people have equal access to food and healthcare. Suppose you were to build institutions that essentially "compete" with the mainstream delivery of food and healthcare services, because those services aren't working. This too is a window.

Throughout the 1970s, the Black Panther movement gained national attention, often because of what the media described as their militancy. Too few people noticed that they were also serving pancake breakfasts on Sunday mornings to young people struggling with hunger, operating medical clinics to serve those who couldn't afford to see a doctor, and conducting other public services that were not being performed by the government. All it took to legitimize the Black Panther movement in contrast to the White-dominant United States government in the eyes of thousands of Americans was a consistent and genuine concern for the health and well-being of Black people. It was a glimpse into an alternate society.

Resilient Coders is one small member of a community of people and organizations working to build an alternate vision of the way people build wealth. We operate in protest of the current caste system, in which a person must be born into privilege in order to gain more privilege. We know that there are exceptions, but we understand them as such; they're aberrations in a system built to favor stasis, with those on top staying on top, and those on the bottom struggling more for less. We envision a parallel economic reality, built out of parallel structures, in which a person's professional success is actually reflective of their ambition and work ethic.

The nonprofit workforce development industry has emerged to provide the services that aren't otherwise being addressed by either the public or private sectors. It's important work. Those services are essential, like a tourniquet is essential to slow the bleeding from an open wound. But the wound is still open, and the tourniquet is inadequate. We need to wake up to the fact that bandaging is not the same as healing. Nonprofit services don't have the power to end the injustices that make them necessary. Service without protest is not enough.

We've been dealing with company cultures we know to be toxic and racist. We've been working with managers who believe learning and growth are tasks for other people. We *know* we're grabbing our people by the ankles and flinging them over the ramparts into environments that will likely be hostile to them. We tend to respond by preparing our students to brace for a rough landing. At what point do we storm the castle?

Disruption of the industry is possible.

These ideas don't seem that radical on paper: All people deserve an equal shot at prosperity. All of us must be captains of our own professional destinies, free to determine the contours of our own trajectories. The direction those trajectories take, their nature, their profitability, and the pace at which they advance must be determined by factors that are within our control, not by any confines imposed on us by the constructs or conditions into which we're born. The harder you work, the more you earn. Such is the dream of meritocracy.

It is, for many people, the dream that remains a dream. This is a book about race and wealth, but we must also acknowledge that there are other dimensions of exclusion as well, also based on circumstances that are beyond a person's control. These may include gender identity and expression, sexual orientation, neurodivergence, or physical disabilities, among others. These folx, their stories, and the contexts in which they operate deserve more attention than we can give in a book with as narrow a scope as this one.

Specifically regarding the economic conditions under which people are born, it follows that, if we want a true meritocracy, pathways into high-growth careers must not be determined by those economic conditions. We must all have access to free education that is the same quality as expensive education. Money does not delineate the quality of education in a system in which we all have meritocratic access to prosperity. Money cannot determine the relevance of the curriculum to industry needs, nor can it be exchanged for social capital. Any system in which free education is inferior to expensive education in its ability to connect graduates with high-paying jobs is a system rife with injustice.

In a just system, the onus of paying for training does not fall on the student. Payment must be the responsibility of an external entity, such as a government agency or the employer. Subsidized education is unlikely to come from the government right now, because we have elected to chronically underfund public education. There's a history to this. Heather McGhee chronicles much of it in her book *The Sum of Us*. A wave of conservatism swept through

White America in the late seventies and early eighties, during which state budgets were slashed and public amenities defunded. State universities, once a model of economic mobility, became unaffordable to most students, particularly to Black students, whose parents and grandparents had not been allowed to benefit from the postwar boom. The chasm between most prospective students and access to a college education is still widening today. In the forty years following the passage in 1979 of Proposition 13, which capped property taxes in California, tuition at the state's public colleges increased eightfold.[4] There's no reason to suspect or hope that this trend to defund will end anytime soon.

There's no plausible macroeconomic argument that supports the slashing of publicly funded education. Economic mobility is good for tax revenue, and it's great for business. That's why, in other parts of the world, the most competitive universities are free. The chronic underfunding of economic mobility is an American phenomenon, with American roots.

It began as a backlash to the civil rights movement, when White Americans perceived a reversal in the government's historic role in legitimizing and enforcing structures of White supremacy. Before then, expansive investments in economic development were generally popular and bipartisan, as they worked to uphold the existing racial hierarchy. The GI Bill of 1944, for example, sent a generation of White veterans to college—and Black veterans to segregated vocational schools. That program was popular with White voters. But once the federal government appeared to step into a role of upending rather than upholding the racial hierarchy, it suddenly became the enemy and needed to be restrained. White Southerners abandoned the party of Kennedy and Johnson in favor of the party promising law and order and fiscal responsibility. Both of these political platforms were racial dog whistles, crafted by strategists with the explicit intention of peeling White laborers away from the party of labor, on the basis of their deeply ingrained racism. It worked then as a political device. It continues to work today.

To the extent that the United States can be called a representative democracy, it is representative of a culture unwilling to support a sustained push for justice. We're too susceptible to misinformation that validates our prejudices; this is why in American political discourse, facts are the garnish, not the steak.

If we are ever to approach the fabled American meritocracy, we need grand sweeping change to come from Washington, and in order for that to happen, we will first need grand sweeping change in mainstream American culture. We'll be waiting for a dream to come true so that another dream can come true so that a third dream can come true. I'd rather we just wake up. No more waiting for the cavalry; it's not coming. Rent is due at the end of the month. We need action now. Not Twitter rants; not corporate pledges, nor strongly worded emails to the whole company calling everybody White supremacists. It doesn't put bread on any tables. We need to build parallel structures that bypass the "traditional" college-to-tech pipeline in which you need to have a lot of money to make a lot of money. Nobody will build them except those of us who choose to build them.

We need training models that are both free to workers and accountable to them. Power must be squarely in the hands of those most directly affected. The fates of large groups of people cannot be determined by anyone other than themselves. Some enterprises have begun conducting their own training for all entry-level software developers. It makes sense. Robust onboarding efforts save a tech company time and money, by shortening the amount of time it takes a new developer to start contributing meaningfully to the team's output. Such training also gives the employer an opportunity to inculcate in the employee not just general technical aptitudes but also the company's specific processes, workflow, and culture. It's not just about shipping code the right way but rather shipping code in a way that works best at that particular company. Normalizing processes saves time and minimizes confusion.

Some states have begun experimenting with tech apprenticeship models. While the specifics of the model seem to vary state to state, and sometimes even within a single state, the general idea is this: An employer commits to hiring a student full time who completes the training, which is offered by an outside provider. Training is free to the student and features a hybrid approach of learning and working. The employer pays the training provider once the student is hired. The state's Department of Labor contributes to that compensation, sometimes paying the training provider directly and other times offering tax breaks to the employer, once the employer has compensated the training provider.

The apprenticeship model has potential, with some tweaks. Currently many apprenticeships require entrance exams, which overwhelmingly skew White, male, and college-educated. They don't usually offer stipends, which excludes those who can't afford to leave the workforce for several months of training before the work portion of their apprenticeship begins. Once these details have been ironed out, apprenticeships may represent one of a plurality of viable equitable paths to prosperity.

For any pathway into the workforce to be equitable, we must understand what is equitable and what is not equitable. This cannot be decided by enterprises. It can't come exclusively from the chief diversity officer, whose perspective on the hiring of Black and Brown people is necessarily corporatist, per her accountability to a corporation. It can't be up to the content marketing department, as they draft the "values" content on the corporate website and schedule the tweets. As is always the case, that which affects the people must be led by the people. Otherwise, this is all an elaborate exercise in speaking on behalf of others.

We need a body of principles. Those principles must be drafted by members of the communities that have been largely excluded from tech, disproportionately Black, Indigenous, and Latinx. They must be allowed to evolve over time, adapting to the ever-changing needs of the space. And most importantly, there must be a system of accountability. Without accountability, principles are just words. Theory without practice.

The development of these principles, their continued evolution, and the advancement of their application in practice is the work of an institution that doesn't yet exist in tech, to my knowledge. This is a council, composed not of enterprises but of workers. It operates independently of traditional institutions of power like enterprises and government, accountable only to the people it represents.

No body of principles is worth the kilobytes it occupies if it's not applied in practice. The principles don't matter. The council doesn't matter, nor do its members. Its organizational structures and processes don't matter. Nothing matters but the demonstrable shift in the lived experiences of real people. If it doesn't help pay the rent, it doesn't matter.

Resilient Coders, and the broader community of organizations to which we belong, could convene a congress to draft principles and vote them into canon. That's easy. But until we have the means by which to agitate for the adoption of those principles throughout the industry, such a congress will be an academic exercise. We'd be writing a document that lives on someone's computer, maybe gets as much exposure as a link from an article, and is then forgotten.

This is the only reason why corporate diversity, equity, and inclusion policies matter to me: This broader push must be led by

Black and Latinx techies, but there are too few of us right now to do this alone. If we begin the push now, all we'd be doing is making ourselves vulnerable at work. When the lone Black or Latinx techie makes noise, that's one person in violation of the corporate code of conduct. When there are many, the corporate code of conduct is in violation of the person. We can't agitate until there are more of us. And there won't be more of us until we agitate.

Right now, the only way forward is solidarity across all peoples.

Solidarity is a myth we may or may not choose to believe in.

Not everyone agrees that genuine solidarity exists or that it is even possible. It's not a given that someone from among an empowered community, such as a cisgender heterosexual White man, has any role whatsoever to play in the revolutionary activities of those who struggle against the social and economic dominance of cisgender heterosexual White men. In fact, there are those who would argue that the entire concept of solidarity is a fabrication.

Of course it's a fabrication. And so is matrimony. So are the concepts of society, of right and wrong, and of the United States of America. They're only real insofar as enough of us choose to believe they're real. The question of whether or not solidarity can ever be objectively "real" doesn't matter, since there is no such thing as objective reality in matters of personal conviction. That's the wrong framework through which to approach solidarity, since there's nothing objective, quantifiable, or empirical about it. Just like the United States, I can't prove that it exists, beyond proving that there are other people who also believe it exists. It's a construct, existing entirely within the minds of the people thinking about it. Trying to prove the existence of solidarity is the same as trying to prove the existence of God. Just the act of bringing it into the arena of objective debate makes the whole thing dissolve.

Federal law is another such social construct. My belief in its existence changes the way I behave. Other people's belief in federal law *also* changes the way I behave. If other people didn't believe so fervently in federal law that they could significantly change or even end my life, it wouldn't exist.

Solidarity similarly crosses over from personal conviction to "reality" in the form of action. If it doesn't change the way we behave, it doesn't exist.

Solidarity starts with requiring more than platitudes.

"Black Lives Matter" as a corporate token of solidarity is the Left's version of the Right's "thoughts and prayers" after a school shooting. I care, but not enough to do anything about it. I care, throughout the duration of the media cycle. I care, as long as it costs me no money, no time, no political or social capital, and no difficult self-reflection. I care, as long as my position at this company, and within our broader social power structure, remains absolutely intact. I care, as long as it doesn't involve me at all. I care enough to hope that someone else fixes it. I care enough to say that I care.

Empty words are an important part of appeasing the people whose buy-in is required to maintain existing structures of power. We want our existing narratives confirmed. We want to be heard, affirmed, and comforted. And when we are satiated, we nod and move on. When the crisis is abstract to you, so is the solution. When you're thrust into the fight by the trauma of reading headlines, you're cured with the balm of reading happier headlines. You leave the fight.

This is why one of the greatest threats to activism is "slacktivism." When tweeting allows people to believe that they've done the work, they don't go any further. Slacktivism removes from the theater of battle those who otherwise might have made the greatest warriors. Self-righteous inaction is more of a threat to progress than total apathy.

Corporate public statements are a form of orchestrated corporate slacktivism. They'll continue to work, as long as it's enough for you, the worker. As long as such statements make workers feel better, corporations are required to do nothing more.

Another popular form of corporate slacktivism is the mandatory participation in corporate diversity trainings. Often called "Diversity, Equity, and Inclusion" (DEI), "Diversity, Equity, Inclusion, and Belonging" (DEIB), or "Diversity, Inclusion, Equity, and Justice" (DIEJ), the acronyms range, but the outcomes are nearly identical: they don't lead to material changes in the racial demography of a workplace or to a change in workplace culture. In fact, they often backfire. In a piece titled "Why Diversity Programs Fail," the *Harvard Business Review* notes, "The positive effects of diversity training rarely last beyond a day or two, and a number of studies suggest that it can activate bias or spark a backlash."[5]

Diversity, Equity, and Inclusion is generally not an industry that holds itself accountable for the achievement of real progress toward diversity and equity. If it were, its clients in tech and in other industries would expect some degree of measurable progress. They don't. Typically, they're not even clear on what it is they should be measuring.

Imagine paying for a service without having any way of measuring whether or not the service actually worked.

Corporate clients often don't know what DEI training is supposed to do. They just know that they need to do it. This is the problem with trainings with this particular focus: There is seldom consensus around the objective of the trainings, and so they devolve into collective navel-gazing, acknowledgments of privilege, and acceptance of complicity in structural racism. It's true that change begins within each individual. But in these trainings, there it stays. All the White people admit their guilt and then go back to processing email. In the more progressive meetings, they also acknowledge the Indigenous people from whom the land they stand on was forcibly taken. And *then* they go back to processing email.

It's not uncommon for a company to arrive at the conclusion that "diversity" has nothing to do with the way they hire. In these cases, issues of racial justice are sidelined to outlets that are more accessible both culturally and financially, such as paid volunteering time, product discounts to nonprofits, and the classic awkward effort to be more "inclusive" in the promotion of their public events. This happens all the time at Resilient Coders: a company won't interview an alum for an open role for which the alum is amply qualified, but the company would like to invite them to their events. That's neither diversity, nor equity, nor inclusion.

Often the company determines that they want more people of color to work there, but they are wholly uninterested in changing who and how they recruit. This is like hoping to lose weight without changing your behavior. The scale will keep presenting the same truth every time you step on it.

Training without a goal, in any context, is an elaborate act of theater. To people of color trying to break into tech, diversity trainings are a tragicomedy. At Resilient Coders, we watch from the outside with our noses pressed against the glass while White tech workers call each other White supremacists, and our résumés continue to stream past them like the distant hum of traffic.

To the folx whose résumés are being ignored, it doesn't matter what the book club is reading. They don't care whether or not the CEO posted a statement on LinkedIn. They're not following your company on Twitter, they're not impressed with the Black Lives Matter graphic, and they are uninterested in attending the company's "diversity hackathon." They just want the job. They want to be evaluated fairly.

We are in the midst of a crisis of power disparity. There is only one metric that matters in the evaluation of our efforts: To what extent are you recalibrating the balance of power?

Don't hand me a glass of water from your reservoir when you have the power to break the dam.

Power accumulates. So does dispossession. Consider the traditional power plant, built alongside a river. It requires a dam. In a way, the dam is itself powerful, in that it exerts control over the actual source of power. It allows the plant to maximize the derivation of power from the river by the measured restriction and redirection of the flow of water. In short, at the plant, power is maximized by the degree to which the flow of water is restricted. Power is extracted and hoarded by those who own the dam. Someone possesses, and someone else is dispossessed.

Dispossession by the powerful is an old trope, and it's been explored at length. In his essay "The 'New' Imperialism: Accumulation by Dispossession," David Harvey describes the confiscation of public property and its subsequent privatization, such that a privileged few benefit at the expense of the many.[6] He is writing about the late eighties, a period of overt confederation between government officials and corporate interests to deploy public resources for private gain. They were producing dispossession, the separation of people from that which is rightfully theirs. This both requires and exacerbates the diminution of power held by the public. It's not hard to see this process in action today, especially since the Supreme Court's ruling in Citizens United in 2010 that corporations can spend unlimited money on political activity. The auctioning off of our elected leaders and their influence is an example of the dispossession of public resources that begets more dispossession of public resources.

While federal governments around the world have proven to be effective agents of dispossession, they're not necessary for the practice to flourish. Sociologist Charles Tilly introduces the term "opportunity hoarding" to describe practices through which dispossession is exercised by one class over another.[7] It's not that there exist those who have and those who have not, operating in isolation from each other. Rather, there exist those who have *because* there are those who have not, and racism is fundamental to the continued perpetuation of this dynamic. Like the dam that controls the river for the benefit of the few, so too do those in power control access to opportunity.

Subsequent studies have examined inequalities in various arenas through the lens of opportunity hoarding. It's particularly evident, and its impact might be especially consequential, in education. A recent study from a team of educational researchers, "Does STEM Stand Out?," notes that tech culture is exclusionary precisely because the field represents a reliable gateway to prosperity. It begins with a synopsis of earlier studies that focus on opportunity hoarding in K–12 schools before it turns to higher education. The authors note that "a clear example of opportunity hoarding emerges when groups create social advantages through some form of educational segregation and, thus, essentially gain control of education as a highly valuable resource."[8]

Cultures of exclusion develop when the stakes are high. Even when the resources in question are not necessarily scarce, they're hoarded and *made* scarce. It's an old story: Whether it's gold, oil, rushing water, or education, resources that offer a path to wealth are routinely seized and kept away from others. They're made scarce because their scarcity makes them valuable. We value expensive education precisely because it's exclusionary.

And yet, we need to feel as though we earned our wealth, that we are somehow more deserving of it than others. In education, this means believing that you and your friends who graduated with expensive degrees are more worthy of those degrees than those without them. At scale, it means believing that entire groups of people are more worthy than other entire groups of people.

Tech culture is imbued with tropes and stereotypes about who is and who is not worthy of opportunity. Those tropes and stereotypes perform the explicit function of controlling access. Hoarding doesn't necessarily manifest as active resistance, but rather as passive dismissal.

The authors of the study note that within universities, the rate of persistence among Black and Latinx students pursuing STEM-related majors is proportionally low compared with that of their White and Asian peers. This model accounts for variations in academic preparedness. Simply put, the data highlights the notable rate at which STEM-related majors repel Black and Latinx students specifically, for reasons unrelated to aptitude. The culture of exclusion to which Black and Latinx students are routinely subjected is particularly rampant in tech.

There's a gulf between the socially progressive values that the majority of urban techies profess and the persistence of racial disparities endemic in our industry. It's an odd dichotomy: anti-racist sentiment seems especially high, but the proportion of Black and Latinx hires remains especially low. Why?

Opportunity hoarding offers one explanation: White and Asian techies might have no overt or conscious animosity toward Black or Latinx people, until they're competing with them for a job. Then the biases begin. *She's smart, but come on now—is she really smarter than I am?*

The awkward intellectual peacocking that we've all been dismissing for decades with a roll of the eyes as "nerd culture" is symptomatic of opportunity hoarding. When you need to believe that you're the smartest person in the room for the sake of your own peace of mind, it becomes necessary to depress everyone else's intellect. You need to be able to quickly dismiss people as inferior. Especially when confronted with a potential competitor, you need to be able to afford yourself some paternalistic safety: *I think you're great, but . . . you, in this role?* Racist and sexist stereotypes are useful psychological tools with which to elevate oneself above competitors. And not all tools are deployed intentionally.

At Resilient Coders, opportunity hoarding appears during our sales process. It's a regular feature in our early conversations with some of our new prospective employers, manifesting as an assumption that our alumni couldn't possibly do the work. "We love what you're doing, but . . . here? This challenging and highly technical role, at *this* company?"

Yes. This challenging and highly technical role, at this company.

Our alumni have the ability to overcome this deficit, and they routinely do so. The point is that they shouldn't have to start from a deficit. It shouldn't be entirely on them.

I once believed that the only viable response to the opportunity hoarding we experience is an overwhelming display of talent. If the bar is unreasonably high, we will jump unreasonably high. But as our community of alumni and allies within the industry continues to grow, it's time to adopt a new approach. *You* do some of the work. *You* who keep the dam, restricting resources in order to generate power for yourselves: join us in dismantling it.

Are your company's "diversity and inclusion" efforts working to recalibrate power? Or are you handing out glasses of water from your reservoir?

CHAPTER 5

YOU HAVE THE POWER
TO BREAK THE DAM

YOUR TECH COMPANY'S CEO has authority, but her authority is not necessarily equal to her power. They're different. Authority is granted to her and supported by other systems of authority. She has the authority to fire you, and she can terminate your payroll. The payroll company acknowledges her authority to fire you and will honor her request to remove you from the payroll. If you were to challenge your termination in a court of law, the judge would acknowledge that she has the authority to fire you. She can also confer that authority on another person—a CTO, a human resources professional—and by extension *that* individual has the authority to fire you.

Authority is inherent in your CEO's role. It's a figment of the corporate structure we all generally subscribe to. But power, on the other hand, is not inherent. She has power because you and your colleagues grant her that power—mainly through your company's continued success. Commercial success engenders the trust of powerful people: investors, more employees, and consumers. It is a font of power that can be open and shut like a spigot by employees.

In addition to achieving commercial success, brands are increasingly under pressure to represent social values as well. Visible corporate values are important to contemporary consumers, particularly to millennials and younger, who collectively represent a sizable and vocal segment of the consuming public and will do so for decades to come. We're increasingly expecting brands to wade into the fray of social and political issues and to make showy public expressions of values. Employees increasingly want to feel as though their work, and the bulk of their waking time, is contributing to the advancement of their values. None of us wants to feel as though our hard work is actively making the world a worse place.

In tech especially, there is a culture of collective effort for collective gain. At organizations like Code for America, programmers volunteer to build applications for public use, often competing with each other for the honor of having built the most beneficial bit of software.

Members of the open-source community advocate for software that is free, transparent, and open to public contribution—think of Wikipedia for programmers—as an act of resistance against the encroachment of proprietary interests on public assets, such as the internet, and the increasingly dubious behavior of tech companies. If you use the browser Mozilla Firefox, for example, you are benefiting from the work of a vast network of programmers volunteering their time to ensure that internet access remains free and unfettered.

If you and your colleagues are good at what you do and hard to replace, the CEO at your company wants you to stay there. She'll want you to be happy at work. She'll want to make it clear to you that whatever you're doing is in alignment with your social values, that by working there, you're fulfilling your self-identity: you're making the world a better place. The CEO's power comes from your consent to work for her. Your consent continues as long as you believe in what you're doing. Your belief in what you're doing, a belief shared with your colleagues, is part of the bedrock underlying your company culture, underpinning your "common sense." It's the root of your structuration. It's the filter through which you experience new events and weave them into a narrative that supports your identity. It's the bond you have with your colleagues. It's what keeps you working hard today and dreaming of tomorrow's shared victories. It's hard to imagine a task more important to a CEO than the cultivation of a company culture in which employees want to participate. Without that, they have little power to influence their workers.

It's up to you as the employee to determine what does or does not earn your buy-in. Our contacts at tech companies often tell us that hiring differently is "just not a priority for the CEO right now." Sometimes it's presented in defense of the CEO; more often it's a grievance. Regardless, it's almost universally true. It's not a priority, because the CEO's job is to prioritize the commercial success of the business. Your company probably does not exist for the purpose of advancing social justice. The CEO's entire function within the organization is to develop strategies by which to make the company money and allocate the resources necessary to execute those strategies efficiently. For the CEO, the company's social and civic impact is a secondary concern at best, with a few notable exceptions, after its commercial milestones. Secondary concerns don't often get done, or they don't get done well.

This is not a moral judgment. A CEO operates under certain pressures. There are plenty of leaders who care deeply about social issues but see a limit as to how much they can realistically accomplish. Their sole professional function, and the goal against which their work is evaluated, is to make the company increasingly more money than it spends. Your CEO might be the most socially conscious CEO in the world, but if she's not making the company more than it spends, she won't be CEO for long. For an employee to expect something else to matter more to the CEO than remaining the CEO is to miss an opportunity to read the landscape of power. It's like sailing without knowing which direction the wind is coming from.

A CEO is bound by her situation within a broader landscape of power. She might agree with your position to some degree. Your campaign might actually be personally important to her. She might also, however, feel powerless to effect cultural change in the way and to the extent that you believe necessary. In a sense, it doesn't really matter to your campaign whether or not that's actually true. If what you're hoping to do is find common ground with this person, it's important to start by understanding their perspective on the landscape of power.

This is irrespective of what they actually say. Someone's perspective on their own situation within a broader landscape of power is not always accurate. They may misunderstand their own situation, and even if they do understand it, they may have reasons to misrepresent it to you. Those reasons could be strategic, or they could be human. We all feel fear, trepidation, a need to mitigate risk, and the desire to be validated and respected. The way a person describes what they can and can't do is a datum.

It's a mistake to focus on whether or not your campaign is a priority for the CEO. That misses the point. What matters is whether or not it's a priority for you and your colleagues. High on the docket of initiatives that *are* a priority for the CEO is earning your buy-in. It's on you to set your price. If you and your colleagues are okay with empty platitudes, you will get empty platitudes. If you're comfortable with public statements of solidarity but don't care much for action, you will get public statements of solidarity and no action. If you require some sort of token gesture, you will get a token gesture and no more. The CEO will generally push only as hard as you demand that she push, especially if these efforts represent a departure from her other responsibilities.

Coalition

Want only one thing. Every effort to organize must arrive at, and rally around, an objective so simple it can be printed on a sticker. *Fight for $15. Love is love. No uno más.*

Coalitions are built around shared purpose. Find your people among your colleagues. Communicate regularly, ideally using platforms or processes you're already familiar with, but being careful with anything you write down. Be especially wary of writing to each other on a platform that could be monitored, such as your company's email or Slack instance.

If you do have some means of structured or scheduled communication, balance it out with more organic and spontaneous conversation as well. You won't all agree on everything. That's fine. Listen to each other. Understand the nature of your disagreements. These shouldn't be debates but explorations. Don't try to "lead" the effort alone. Equity is about the recalibration of power. Be cognizant of the power dynamics you're building within your coalition. This requires a certain degree of intention, since power dynamics are inherent to any assembly of people.

Your goal with these early conversations is to identify the gap between equitable employment practices and what your company is doing. Write down what you want. Use as few words as possible. Everyone who identifies with your group, if randomly prompted, must be able to adequately articulate in a single sentence the coalition's objective. The whole choir needs to be singing from the same songbook.

Be as disciplined as you can with the specific corollary points you're fighting for. And be clear about what action you want leadership to take. If your goal is nebulous or if the path to its achievement is not clear, your campaign will fall apart. If you say, "We need to be more inclusive in the way we recruit," for example, you need to be able to articulate an actionable goal and the steps by which the goal must be achieved.

Once you and your colleagues know what you want, the purpose of your early conversations is to answer three core questions:

1. Who are the influential people we need to bring to our side?
2. What's stopping them?
3. What do we do about it?

These questions will determine the contours of your next phase.

Every company is different, but generally speaking, you shouldn't need to wait very long before you start bringing members of leadership into these conversations. Frame the discussion as a desire to learn from them, and treat it as such. Start by asking, rather than telling. Assume there's a bigger picture that you're not privy to. Why is it that we do it this way and not that other way? The strongest arguments are made entirely with respectful but probing questions. If you pull at the right thread, the sweater unravels.

Treat your CEO like a partner, implying that you know they share your values and believe in your campaign. It might even be true. Ask, for example, "What are our potential blockers, given that we both want to be hiring differently?"

These are the most common deflections we see, during early conversations about changing corporate recruitment practices, between a company's leadership and the employee pushing for change:

We don't have time right now.

Okay. When will be the right time? What key indicator will signal that we're ready? Is it about revenue? Whatever it is, let's build a path to get there. We need to be able to communicate to staff that we're taking action, and that it will be quantifiable.

We don't have the capacity to support entry-level folx.

Okay. How can we get to the point where we can? When will we know when that is?

Incidentally, if your team really is so strapped all the time that you can't ever collectively assume the two or three hours a week it takes to on-ramp and adequately support a new employee, you might have deeper issues. Your work isn't working for workers, and you should get out.

This other person or group of people will never approve it.

This might be the specific hiring manager or the talent acquisition team or some other member of leadership, and they might simply be deflecting responsibility. But it's also possible that what they're saying is actually true. This is especially common at bigger enterprises, where bureaucracy exists for the purpose of maximizing homogeneity and replicability of processes, at the expense of experimentation or autonomy. Either way, the answer is the same: Who, then, should we be talking to? Let's bring them into the conversation and find out what their blockers are.

When a leader insists that they agree with you in theory, it's just that there are certain logistical challenges, you can take the position that since you're on the same page, you want to understand the logistical challenges and be a part of removing them.

There are two types of resistance you'll meet from those at the levers of power, once you start asking questions. A colleague of mine in workforce development has names for these people: There's the *Don't Wanna* and the *Don't Know How.* Neither of them will ever self-identify as such. It's incumbent on you to recognize them and treat them accordingly.

The Don't Know How will sometimes masquerade as a Don't Wanna because it's embarrassing to them to not know something. Pull them in. Treat them as the future allies they are.

The Don't Wanna might masquerade as a Don't Know How because it's easier than admitting to a colleague that you just don't care that much about equitable employment practices. Recognize them and move on. You're not out to change minds at this point. And if all you have at your company are those you can identify as Don't Wanna, get out.

Be a person who takes the time to understand a plurality of perspectives on any issue. This is hard. It is itself an act of resistance in the context of a society that demands that we all select one of two complete systems of sociopolitical ideology and swallow it whole into our self-identity. May we all strive to be so comfortable with ourselves that we don't feel the need to subscribe to the ideological value pack assigned to us by someone else. And may we stay humble enough and strong enough to keep faith in our own capacity to keep learning from others.

You will need this strength while speaking to someone outside your coalition with whom you disagree. But you will need it much more when speaking to someone *within* your coalition with whom you disagree. This is much harder and, ultimately, more important. Approach every disagreement with the expectation that you will learn something. You probably will, even if it's not necessarily what the speaker intended. If and when you listen and continue to disagree, at least you now disagree more intelligently.

Disagreements may become uncomfortable at times, but they don't need to descend into openly hostile conflict. And if they do, be careful about how you manage that conflict and how you communicate through it. We've used the circle process to navigate a series of challenging conversations at Resilient Coders. It's a gathering during which participants talk about potentially difficult or uncomfortable topics within certain guidelines. It's meant to be egalitarian, respectful, and honest. If you're curious about leading your own circle, Mediators Beyond Borders International offers some great information that might be helpful.[1] One of our alumni brought this resource to our attention.

You might not be able to bring your company's leadership into a conversation right away. The most likely scenario is that they offer a token and then disappear. This means you're too low on their priority list. It may be time to catapult yourself to the top.

There is no playbook for escalation. It all depends on what works for your company, your situation, and your own situational assets and challenges. The only consistent threads are the demonstration of popular support throughout the company, the fact that you're collectively difficult and expensive to replace, and the clear and consistent communication of the group's tangible, quantifiable, and feasible demand to leadership.

This is where your understanding of the landscape of power is important. The people you need to convince are ultimately accountable to someone. This might be an empowered entity within the organization, such as a boss or a board of directors. More commonly, it's some combination of employees, consumers, and the general public. While specific tactics vary, successful campaigns tend to threaten to disrupt the relationships of trust on which your company's leadership rests. You may exercise a display of solidarity throughout your workforce, for example, such as a petition or a walkout. If this is your path, remember to always allow your leadership the opportunity to save face and regain your group's trust and respect. This is not out of the goodness of your heart; it's a necessary piece of your action. Pressure is propulsive only if there's a way out; you have the chance to design what that is.

If more pressure is necessary, you may choose to appeal to the general public through public messaging. This method works only if the general public will actually care. Caring is not always our strength as a species, especially not right now. We all have a ton of other issues to be incensed about, and your company's internal processes are unlikely to be a priority. There are a few key people who might care: Potential candidates for jobs, key customer segments, and prospective partners concerned with their own reputations. Their opinions matter deeply to your company's leadership. The more targeted you are with your messaging, the more likely it is to make an impact.

As always, don't make yourself easy to dismiss by being an ass. Avoid indulging in righteous indignation. Don't be a landmine, exploding under the slightest bit of pressure. The world has enough people who are too fragile for disagreement. Don't join them.

Some folx struggle with trauma. If you're among them, and you're not confident that you can have this conversation without compromising your wellness, don't do it. Prioritize yourself.

If you just can't have a conversation with someone you disagree with because it's an affront to your progressive values, you've misunderstood the meaning of the word "progress."

Be who you authentically are. There is strength in that.

CHAPTER 6

REBUILDING

ENDING THE PAY-TO-PLAY workforce system in America, in which we need to spend a lot of money before we can make a lot of money, is a necessary first step in any journey toward economic justice. But it's only a first step, just one dimension of at least three that are in need of radical transformation: To rebuild a new, more equitable workforce, we must also transform the ways in which we train workers and examine the cultures of the spaces in which we are trying to include new workers. We need to fundamentally overhaul both vocational education and culture.

"Vocational education" does not refer necessarily to a school. Education doesn't have to be a function that is performed exclusively at educational institutions, by professional educators, in isolation from the rest of the world. Ours is a society that quarantines education. We have buildings for that, designed to contain educational activities. We have specialists, who have themselves spent years in seclusion, preparing to perform discrete acts of education inside educational institutions for the supposed benefit of students whose exclusive function is to sit in chairs and be the passive recipients of those acts. Students are blank canvases on which others perform their work. And once the oeuvres are completed, they are dismissed from the educational institution. That chapter of their lives is over forever, unless they choose to further quarantine.

It's important to note that we did not arrive at a quarantine model of education because of its superiority over other competing models. Education is a commodity like any other commodity in a capitalist context: Its value is predicated on its scarcity. It's a resource to be hoarded. There's no place in our cultural understanding of the word "education" for learning that is free, spontaneous, public, and uncredentialed. It would be a threat to our entire social hierarchy, which persists intergenerationally thanks in part to prohibitively expensive education.

We institutionalize education so that we can sell it.

In tech, we prefer to hire people whose educational journeys have been more expensive than other candidates' journeys, precisely *because* they were more expensive. We support the continued inflation of the cost of education. We hoard opportunity. We assume, based on no evidence, that a candidate from a private university is better than a candidate from a public university and that both are better than an autodidact without a degree. The person who didn't need to spend any money to arrive at the same interview for the same job is the one we dismiss right away. What value could she possibly offer?

The necessary first step to stopping this scenario from occurring again is, of course, to make top-notch education completely free, as it is in other parts of the world. But we must go further. Education must also be released from quarantine. We need to support and normalize continued learning, indefinitely and everywhere. For the sake of economic justice, education must be expected to persist at work.

Vocational training

The next phase after we ditch pedigree-based hiring in tech will be a broader adoption of skills-based hiring. This is still a model that centers standardized testing, and it has its community of advocates who are optimistic that standardized testing can be done with minimal bias. If that's possible, I haven't seen it yet. Hiring managers can still choose the questions that are asked. This seems like it's rife with opportunities for bias. Standardized tests will forever favor a particular way of thinking. That's inherently biased. Candidates struggling with imposter syndrome, disproportionately women and people of color, are less likely to perform at their own level on a standardized test relative to white men.[1]

Will this change someday? Maybe. Until then, we must advocate for hiring people who demonstrate potential through project-based assessment and for training them on the job in the discrete skills they need. Some companies are already there. Most are not.

Skills-based hiring as it's currently done in tech tends to test for specific tools, by which I mean programming languages, frameworks, and microservices, rather than transferable skills, such as time management or effective communication. But tools change. Your company will probably migrate to a different set of tools within the next five years. If you've hired a team full of people who are good at the tools you're using right now but not particularly interested in continued skill development, your migration will go poorly. Or worse, it won't happen at all, and your company will limp along like a zombie, holding on to an obsolete tech stack that no one else wants to work on. You won't be able to hire young top talent. At least zombies occasionally get their fresh brains.

We should be hiring for the skills you can't train, and then training for the specific tools needed on the job. If you're hiring an engineer who will be programming in Ruby, for example, hire someone who works hard, believes in continued self-improvement, and is likely to be a positive influence on the people around her. It doesn't matter if she's never programmed in Ruby, which can be learned. Those other skills can't.

We need to apply some longitudinal thinking to the way we hire. The best employee might not be the biggest contributor on the first day of the job. Hire the person you think might be the best contributor in six months. If you can hire someone whose rate of growth looks aggressive, their aptitudes upon entry won't matter for very long.

The commercial argument for training is that what's good for the worker is also profitable for the company, but we need to step away from that intersection. We need to normalize advocating for human beings for no other reason than their humanity. We can support this commercial argument, but there is more power in shedding our need for it.

There is also a social argument for training. If you insist that you need your early-career hires to be able to demonstrate experience in specific tools, you are narrowing your search to the privileged. You will be choosing from people who have enjoyed the privilege of time to code without being paid for it. You will be excluding those who have had to work or who have helped raise their siblings or who don't have the network to be attuned to which programming languages they should be teaching themselves or who are simply unaware of their gifts because they haven't had the time, hardware, or opportunity to stumble across them.

Training on the job helps level the playing field somewhat. If the skills you're looking for when you hire are those that people will have regardless of their privilege, then—with all else being equal—privilege will diminish as a determining factor at this particular point in your process.

If you're reading this book and trying to find your role within a broader effort to shift tech culture, this might be your path. Establish an on-the-job training program at your company. Its purpose must be to eliminate or at least abate the influence of privilege on your selection of early-career employees.

Make training a part of your onboarding process for all early-career developers, across the board. This is a better option than having a particular track that risks othering the "nontraditional" hires, forever branding them as such to their colleagues. Training some and not others enforces a dynamic that doesn't need to be there, one that doesn't go away easily.

Trainees should be paid well. This includes health insurance and benefits, even before they're contributing meaningfully to the product. Not everyone can just afford to be without income and insurance for the duration of the training.

Good on-the-job training has two objectives: First, it standardizes general technical proficiencies. This is not necessarily because some people "know more" than others. In a field with a toolset as diverse as that which you see in tech, with its plurality of programming languages, frameworks, microservices, and workflows, your incoming engineers will collectively look like a Venn diagram of discrete skills that might overlap. You want everyone to be comfortable with the same skills, which means everybody will need to brush up somewhat. And if some people need to brush up more than others, it shouldn't matter at all to the company. That work is being done by the trainee, during the period of time during which the primary expectation of the trainee is to train. Nobody is evaluating athletes by the number of miles they jog before the season starts. All that matters is their performance after opening day.

Critics of on-the-job training complain that early-career engineers coming into the company without discrete skills are a drain on their managers' time. But if your company really doesn't expect managers to spend at least an hour or two a week with their direct reports, if the structure doesn't allow people at all levels to experiment and occasionally fail, and if the culture doesn't assume that people will continue learning regardless of their level of experience, the problem is not the early-career talent. When we hear prospective employers worry that our graduates will be a drain on their managers' time, we thank them silently for waving a huge red flag. We count our blessings for having been spared a toxic work environment, and we happily move on to other companies with better company culture.

That's the second objective of good on-the-job training: It allows a community to imbue in its newest members a shared culture and set of values. These manifest in different ways. Communication is an omnipresent expression of a company's culture. For example, how does someone ask questions at your company? Who are the people to avoid, because they are either judgmental, unhelpful, or prone to gossiping that the new employee is asking questions? At what point in your process of searching for the answer is it appropriate to ask for help? I've known someone who was admonished for asking too many questions, and someone else who was admonished for asking too few. Ironically, they worked for the same company at the same time. Good on-the-job training has the potential to standardize the expectations we have of each other that are slightly different in each team and aren't necessarily written down.

Vocational training can be an act of disruption.

In his wisdom, our managing director of engineering, Leon Noel, built our bootcamp atop a foundation established by Paulo Freire's treatise *Pedagogy of the Oppressed*. The book, first published in Brazil in 1968, made claims that were so bold and so revolutionary that it was banned in much of the Global South during the era of dictatorships in the 1970s. One of the central ideas is this: The oppressed are as capable and as intelligent as their oppressors. They need not be treated as requiring "help" or "guidance," which are dynamics that can lend themselves to inequitable power constructs. This worldview, in which one group of people is needed in order to "save" another group of people, is the intellectual foundation for systems of oppression throughout history. If one person's liberation is dependent on another person's choice, they can never be equals.

Don't succumb to the usual power tropes in your training. For example, it cannot be an act of charity. It cannot fall under Corporate Social Responsibility. When you talk about your training, eliminate the word "help" from your vocabulary entirely. You're not "helping" anyone. Remember the slogan created by Lilla Watson and her fellow Aboriginal rights activists in the 1970s: "If you have come here to help me, then you are wasting your time. But if you have come because your liberation is bound up with mine, then let us work together."[2]

If you participate in your company's training and your function is to empower other people's learning, don't lecture. Listen more than you teach. Approach every relationship in the classroom with the expectation that the people you're talking to might be smarter than you are. Until you believe—really *believe*—that the learner in front of you could someday become your boss if given enough time, all you're doing is "helping." Liberate yourself and the person in front of you from this power construct, which ultimately comes from your own insecurity.

This doesn't mean that you should ignore the power imbalance endemic to your relationship with the learner. Be aware of it. Accept that they're unlikely to be as direct in their communication with you as you might be with them, even if you ask them to be.

If you have the power to fire them, fail them, or otherwise jeopardize their success, being direct with you is a risk. Communicating frankly with you is an act of trust, and they might not have any particular reason to trust you. Your intentions don't matter. Hold space for the people you're working with. Don't expect candor from your direct reports; earn it.

This dynamic illustrates a radical departure from the model of education we all grew up with in America. In too many traditional school settings, education is a one-way funneling of knowledge from teacher to student. There is no collaboration among peers or learning from them. There's no critique of the information. The instructor deposits information into the heads of their pupils, and the pupils do their best to keep it there, intact. The "best" students are those who passively accept as canon everything said by the teacher. They're the ones our system is designed to propel forward. They're graded according to how well they recall facts, and so there's no sense in challenging the legitimacy of those facts or unpacking them in a group setting. Students are recipients of information. We raise databases in this country, grooming them to store data and retrieve it on command. Freire calls this the "banking model" of education.

More than the facts, what the students and the instructor are all learning in the banking model of education is a dynamic of power: I am giving you knowledge, which we have all chosen to accept as unquestionably valid because of my status as a figure of authority. And because of the knowledge that I give you, your life improves. In fact, your life improves in direct proportion to the amount of information I give to you and your willingness to accept it. Your success, and indeed your whole understanding of the world around you, is predicated on my generosity. For you to be successful, I need to continue to be generous, you need to accept my generosity, and you need to continue to trust in me and in the political and social structures that place me above you.

This is the construct that legitimizes dictatorships. It legitimizes colonialism. The people in this relationship cannot be equals. Freire's book rejects such constructs in favor of those that balance power between people in any kind of exchange. For this reason, *Pedagogy of the Oppressed* was banned.

That's not to say that there should be no authority in a classroom. Authority is important; maybe especially with younger students (we work exclusively with adults at Resilient Coders). But authority can take different forms. We need to move past an antiquated mode of education in which everything said by the figure of authority is true simply because it was said by a figure of authority. In those instances, we're attaching truth to a single person. Truth needs to be able to stand on its own, with or without that person. Certainly, good instructors know their subject matter. But the best instructors are those who encourage dissent.

Freire presents an alternative model of education. In the "dialogic model," learning is a mutual dynamic act, like a dialogue. It's the way we learn naturally, through tandem exploration with those around us. We engage with the material, experimenting with it, examining it, drawing conclusions about it, sharing those conclusions with the people around us, challenging each other and ourselves.

It makes sense in an academic setting. By the time you and your classmates are done arguing over whether President Grover Cleveland was right in deploying the United States Army to end the Pullman Strikes of 1894 or whether the outcomes would have been different if Black men had been allowed to join the American Railway Union, you all will have learned more about this country's attitudes toward labor, class, race, and military intervention than if you had just memorized facts. More importantly, you will have developed a different relationship with the content. It's not bestowed upon you. It's not an artifact enshrined in gold behind bulletproof glass that you admire from a distance. It's immediately accessible to you. You can pick it up, turn it over, and see it from all sides. You might return to it in the future and examine it again through older and wiser eyes.

You develop a different relationship with your classmates too. You all are equals in this discussion. No one is automatically right by virtue of their social status. Your success and your interpretation of the world around you does not depend on the generosity of an authority figure. It's not quite independent either, in that you're not learning in a vacuum. Rather, your success is *interdependent*. It's the sort of interdependence that strengthens communities.

Most people we talk to about this topic are surprised that we would use the dialogic model as a way of teaching highly technical skills in a short period of time. They're committed to the banking model of education and insist that in matters of math and science, "facts are facts." You can't arrive at facts through tandem exploration. The most expedient way for a learner to incur knowledge of facts, they say, is for someone else to deposit them in the learner's brain.

But possession of facts is not the same thing as understanding. If the goal of formal education or any kind of training is that students demonstrate the ability to recall facts on a standardized test within a short period of time of having been exposed to those facts, then the banking model of education works—but only for some students. If by contrast we decide that the goal of education is that students understand and retain the material, then the dialogic model of education is more effective. If we decide that education should also ignite curiosity in our students, foment a sense of personal agency over their own intellectual development, and act as a catalyst for the development of social skills among younger people, then the dialogic model of education is the way.

Unlike banking model education, dialogic education persists outside of quarantine. It reflects the way we understand everything about our surroundings. So much of what we learn from our parents and from our peers is experienced through dialogue rather than through the passive acceptance of facts. In professional settings, colleagues learn from each other through exploration and dialogue. Western scientific research is literally an act of tandem exploration: A community of learners at various points in their understanding of a subject engage collaboratively with the material. They observe. They draw conclusions and share those conclusions with the people around them. Their colleagues challenge their conclusions. Nobody distributes standardized tests to see if they understood the material. There are no "assessments" or "challenges." They discuss as peers, they collaborate on a project as peers, and they arrive at an understanding of the material and of each other's relationship with it.

Because your liberation is bound up with mine

Training is a manifestation of your company's culture. Your training will be successful exactly to the extent to which your organization has developed an ethos of mutual benefit: I'm at your side today, as you learn, because I need you to be awesome at this in a few months, and I wholly believe you have the potential to get there. I'm working through regular expressions with you today because you'll need to use them on my team, and soon, all of us will benefit from your contributions. I'm here because I believe you have talents and character traits beyond your technical aptitudes that I value. I'm here both selflessly and selfishly: Someday soon we will depend on each other equally. I'm investing in a whole community that includes us both.

On-the-job training is a great example of the sort of interdependence in education that strengthens communities. It's not hard to apply a version of Lilla Watson's wisdom to this relationship: *If you have come here to help me learn, you're wasting your time. If you've come here because your success is bound up with mine, let's work together.*

Bringing Lilla Watson and her fellow Aboriginal rights activists into the conference room is an indispensable step in the journey toward parity in tech culture. It is one small act of resistance against tech's endemic culture of exclusion and the routine perpetuation of privilege, and it's a call to approach this work with the gravity it deserves. On-the-job training that is equitable and is conducted in an earnest spirit of mutual benefit is part of a broader effort to dismantle the wall that has been keeping people out of your company and others like it. If we see achieving equity as a chore, we will fail to reach our goal. If we see it as an opportunity to show up for each other, it will succeed. So we start by being the kind of people who believe in showing up for each other. We prioritize community.

We must see in those around us a network of reciprocities. We're in reciprocal relationships with each other, and we're also each in a relationship with the community as a whole. If I spend my time teaching you how to set up a database on your machine, I'm investing my time in you, and I'm investing it in the community. This is not the same as a *donation* of my time, per se. A donation is a reflection of my generosity of spirit. It might not necessarily be sustainable for me long-term to continue to donate. Trying to do so would be anti-systemic, in that I'd be working against, rather than with, a system that requires a certain prioritization of all the many demands on my time. It's possible. I know many people who do this. But this is still not a system. I might *donate* my time to a school in a nearby town. They might get me for a Saturday. I'm happy to rake some leaves or pick up some litter, but it's not really my job, and I don't want to make it a habit. On the other hand, an investment of time is different. I would *invest* my time at the school down the street, because I want my neighborhood to be filled with well-educated, gainfully employed people who shop locally and vote. It's okay to be a little selfish. That's what it means to really be in community: I expect some sort of return on my investment. I respect my neighbors enough to depend on them.

People often bristle at this idea of interconnectedness. They reject the notion that our triumphs and our failures are all communal. These are the "individualists," operating under the impression that we all get to choose whether to live as members of a community or as individuals. Tech is full of individualists. It's not that I disagree with their choice; it's that this choice doesn't exist in contemporary America. There is no such thing as an individualist today. There are no more fur trappers living alone off the land in Des Moines. The choice we get is whether or not to acknowledge that we exist in a network of communities. You get to choose whether to assume your responsibilities or to shirk them. Individualists are those who don't see the people on whose shoulders they're standing.

This same false choice between community and individualism exists at work. On-the-job training is an opportunity for an employer to foment a culture of mutual benefit that long outlasts the time spent in the training.

Training is an instrument that develops and supports a culture that already exists at the company. If the culture upon which your training is founded is one of mutual benefit, you'll want to make it a priority to demonstrate and support that culture in the training itself. This takes more than just surrounding your trainees with people who embody the company culture, though that's important too. You'll want to bring that culture into the systems and processes undergirding your training.

A company at which everyone's ideas are evaluated by their merits rather than by the title, race, or gender of the people who voice them should feature a similar dynamic in their training. No one's perspectives should be beyond examination by virtue of their position; rather, material should be discussed, challenged, and explored in groups. Companies that want their teams to work well in groups should train in groups. Companies that want employees to innovate should encourage their trainees to challenge the way things are currently done. Companies that want employees who take ownership and pride in the work they do within their teams should give them an opportunity to do so during the training.

Evaluation of a trainee should be project-based. Standardized testing has no place in on-the-job training, because it has no place in the job. That's just not how people build product, nor is it how people work together. So why is it a prerequisite in determining which people are going to build product and work together? Proponents of standardized testing argue that it's a way to see how people think. Is it? Is it better than walking through a project with someone and hearing them explain and illustrate how they think? And even if it were a good tool for determining how people think, is there only one right way to think at your company?

Standardized assessments are what allow companies who say they no longer require a bachelor's degree to continue to require a BA in practice. They are almost universally testing for skills that have nothing to do with the job, and the questions on the tests are entirely about material taught in college.

It's not hard to see where this propensity comes from. People aren't necessarily maliciously erecting barriers with the intention of keeping people out. Often people erect barriers and then are surprised that those same barriers are keeping people out. Hiring is all an elaborate act of exclusion, in which your objective is to cull one from the many. The sooner you can get down to one person, the more time and money you've saved the business. There's an entire industry built up around this. The more exclusive the pool of candidates you start with, the better. This isn't itself a culture problem; it's a business need. The problem is that when hiring managers aren't really sure what to look for in a candidate, they default to hiring themselves: I need to find someone just like me, whose path has been just like mine. "Diversity" means hiring a Black person with my same background. They need to have taken my path, because my path has made me into the engineer I am today, which is the ideal. My junior-year algorithm design class has fundamentally changed the way I approach programming, so I need to find programmers who are comfortable with algorithm design.

This is how you end up with people sitting in conference rooms in minority-majority cities and insisting that there just aren't enough people of color in the "pipeline." That's because their "pipeline" is welded to local expensive universities, and they're right—there are too few people of color graduating with computer science degrees from expensive universities.

We all do some version of this sorting. We identify some figment of our backgrounds that has been formative to the way we approach our craft, and we try to argue that it's the only way to do the job well. I've done this myself. I read a lot of history, and I believe it makes me better at my job. In fact, I used to believe that it was impossible to do my job well without an understanding of the ways in which systems of oppression have persisted throughout the history of the Americas. I don't believe that anymore. Today I believe that it would be impossible to do my job, *specifically in the way that I do it*, without that historical perspective. But someone else with different strengths could do my job just as well, albeit differently.

Building systems and processes at work can seem like small work in the context of broader economic justice. But the steps toward economic justice in tech exist within the drudgery of office tasking, not without it. This work can be tedious, but the tedium matters. The tedium is the standard unit of progress. It's the brick you happen to have in your hands right now, to be laid next to the one that came before it, so that you can pick up the brick that comes after it and put that one down too. The labor of organizing people, in just about any context, is not about breathless speeches. Speechmaking is cheap. Real change is work. Want the work.

You'll experiment. You'll occasionally fail, and those failures might cost you a few allies. You might pivot and push in a new direction. You might find yourself wondering, more than once, what all of the effort is for.

You might have your own reasons for doing this work, and that's important. But there's a bigger picture too. As you go about the work of laying brick after brick, remember that there are others doing the same, elsewhere. There are other walls rising on other new buildings. There are other people who want what we want, also building, each in their own way. Every day the sun comes up on a stronger city.

That's why I do this work. I believe we can shift the culture of an entire industry.

CHAPTER 7

BIG IDEAS

ANY CONSTRUCT IMPLEMENTED for the benefit of a group of people must be led by that group of people. The shift toward a tech culture that is more inclusive of Black and Latinx people must be led by Black and Latinx people. Representation matters. We need more of it.

This is a part of why we do the work that we do at Resilient Coders. It's not just about individual people getting jobs and then launching their careers in isolation; there are no individualists in the Resilient Coders community. We subscribe to a bigger vision, in which the proportion of people of color in tech is great enough to have influence over the culture of the whole industry, nationally. "Be Harriet Tubman," says Leon to new students. "When you realize your own liberation, whatever that might mean to you, go back and bring five more with you."

That's our community, but our community is not nearly enough. This movement is much bigger than Resilient Coders will ever be. We must develop a national network of people of color in tech, with the explicit objective of cultural transformation in tech.

Organizing the organizations

Popular education centers tend to be hubs of revolutionary activity. The Highlander Folk School, established in Tennessee in 1932, was originally part of a labor movement in the South. It was a center of both worker advocacy and adult education, illustrating the truth that advocacy without education is as pointless as education without advocacy in the context of workforce development. No service without action, and no action without service. By the 1950s, the school had wholly committed itself to the civil rights movement. There was no syllabus, no "instructor" purporting to teach from a position of authority or expertise. Learning was dialogic. The convenings were an opportunity to share out and to learn from each other's experiences. These were all people operating in different parts of the country, each in their own city. Today we think of Rosa Parks, Septima Clark, Dr. Martin Luther King Jr., Esau Jenkins, and so many others as members of a single monolithic national movement. But movements begin locally. They had to meet each other first, and many of them met at the Highlander Folk School.

Sometimes economic justice in tech seems a long way off. Organizations like ours are all still operating in silos, aware of each other from a distance but without much of a push for meaningful collaboration. One reason for this isolation is a broader generational shift: Much of the social justice work that attracts attention (and money) is being done by nonprofits rather than by activated people who have other jobs. Nonprofits are ultimately businesses operating in a system with other businesses, all of them in competition with each other for revenue and for the job placements or outcomes that demonstrate that we're doing the work we say we do. We might collaborate with each other, but typically those collaborations are peripheral to our core work, and they don't bring us any closer to any of our organizational goals. And for cash-strapped grassroots nonprofit organizations, absolute focus on the organizational goals is an existential necessity.

But there's a second reason for the fragmented landscape. We don't agree with each other. We're not all fighting for the same thing, which is to be expected. Actually, the whole idea of a "movement" as a single spontaneous monolithic uprising in which everyone on the same "side" wants the same thing is an example of the overly simplistic mythmaking we tend to do when recounting our own national history.

The fact is, we all disagree. Those of us in workforce development don't agree on what equitable access to the workforce would actually entail. I have a simple litmus test: I believe equity is measured by the degree to which we're recalibrating power from a place of imbalance to one of balance. Here are some examples of how this manifests: First, money is not a factor in a worker's entrance to a career, nor in her advancement through it. This includes a consideration for the privilege of free time. Paid on-the-job training, along with the removal of the BA requirement in both theory and practice, represents part of a recalibration of power. It's a step toward removing the advantage of wealth at the point of entry to the workforce.

Second, we're talking about salaried, high-paying, in-demand jobs with a growth trajectory. We need to move beyond the idea that "any job is better than no job." It's just not true. Low wages are not enough to live on. A workforce development system that exists for the express purpose of lifting people out of poverty but then routes them to low-wage jobs is not lifting people out of poverty. In such a scenario, it's hard to justify the investment of time that's expected of the participant. And it's not particularly efficient from an economic standpoint if an organization is spending public money to train people for jobs that require them to draw on more public money to survive. The only party that wins in that scenario is the underpaying employer. There is a "foot in the door" argument, with its roots in the very American narrative of starting in the mailroom and working your way up to the corner office. But if the objective of the program is the worker's ascension into the second or third job, then let's build programming that intentionally tracks workers into the second or third job rather than stranding them in the first with nowhere to go.

Third, a recalibration of power requires us to be conscious of existing historical and systemic power inequities. No more trying to ignore them and treating everyone "equally." Poverty is not distributed equally. Barriers to employment are not distributed equally, and conversely, neither is access.

Finally, we need to end our dependence on standardized assessments, as they still favor White male test takers among a set of students with comparable skills. Assessment should be project-based.

Not everyone in the field agrees with these ideas for recalibrating power or with the idea that recalibrating power is in fact the point of workforce development. But there are enough of us who do. The workforce development community is in need of a set of industry standards. We can't expect to push employers in a particular direction together until there is a "together." I'm not suggesting we strive for unity throughout the field; we're not ready for that. Before unity we need to first push for progress. Otherwise "unity" is just an itemized list of what we're already doing, and what we're already doing isn't working.

A subset of us who subscribe to a more equitable vision of workforce access must find each other and speak out in a single voice. This subset must include both practitioners and alumni, since we cannot build structures for workers without workers. We need to delineate what equitable access to the workforce looks like and begin the task of developing a body of principles, perhaps including details from the examples I listed earlier. These principles must be progressive, feasible, and actionable.

As I've said, theory without practice is not enough. We don't need another body of principles that sits on a drive somewhere. What we need is real accountability. No more pledges and platitudes. And we need a way to make the whole thing financially viable without an overdependence on philanthropy. Democratic institutions should ultimately be democratically funded.

Good ideas abound. In "A Design for Workforce Equity," Livia Lam from the Center for American Progress (CAP) introduces the Workforce Equity Trust Fund (WETF). This public policy framework is simple, elegant, and progressive in its reframing of the obstacles to equity It's a refreshing departure from the antiquated "prime the pump" idea, in which the problem is supposedly insufficient or inadequate education. The CAP's plan takes a stand. It focuses on accountability and economic sustainability. It insists that employers must assume some of the expense of training their workforce, which seems only fair.

The plan is predicated on the following four policy pillars, taken directly from the study:

1. Broaden the share of economic risks by requiring employers of a certain size to pay into the WETF
2. Make standard and portable a suite of wraparound services and employment benefits for every worker through the WETF
3. Improve workforce analytics by creating an accountability dashboard for multiple measures of job quality
4. Govern the WETF by a multistakeholder partnership comprising business, labor, and the public[1]

The idea of governance by a multistakeholder partnership is a compelling one. I would argue that people of color in tech deserve their own representation in the partnership, particularly if the issue on the table is their representation in the industry. We need some sort of representative council to fill this role. They could take a seat in a statewide multistakeholder partnership, advocating for more equitable recruitment and employment practices.

Mandating that employers pay for workforce training is another important step toward workforce equity. But it's not enough if there's no incentive to actually hire differently. Existing efforts reveal a gap. For example, employers in Massachusetts pay into a Workforce Training Fund at a rate of 0.056 percent of the wages they pay out. This fund provides state businesses with training grants for incumbent worker training. But it's not enough money, and there's little incentive for those companies to actually hire the workers trained with it.

Boston has a Neighborhood Jobs Trust (NJT) designed to soften the blow of gentrification. When a real estate developer builds in Boston, the developer must pay into this trust. And it's to this trust that nonprofit workforce development organizations like Resilient Coders apply for grants. But there's nothing in the trust legislation incentivizing a company to actually hire people coming out of an NJT-funded organization. The onus of bringing employers to the table is still entirely on the organization. So the various stakeholders in this arrangement and their respective responsibilities and incentives are misaligned. The developer pays and gets nothing in return. The workforce training provider receives some funding for a year, provides training, and is accountable to the city to report job placements. The employer, who is essentially "the client" in this relationship, for whom everyone else is bending over backward, is completely unaware of the entire operation. In traditional client-vendor relationships, the client pays money in exchange for a service. That's not the case with the NJT. Employers by and large get the benefit of workforce development programs for free. Some training providers, including Resilient Coders, charge their employers for their services and are therefore easily undercut by tuition-funded training providers that do not charge the employer. Thus some efforts to alleviate the burden of tuition on students also fail to place the proper onus on the beneficiary, the employer.

We also must put an end to the "cost-savings" value proposition that is rampant in the field. As long as we mean to lure the employers into hiring from workforce development organizations as a way of saving money by insinuating that our workers can be underpaid, we're just creating new constructs of economic oppression. This is the "we're taking a chance on them" argument. From the first day on the job, those workers are entering a relationship in which their value to the company is predicated on being chronically underpaid. That's the banner under which the transaction was made. How do you break out of that pattern, as a worker? How much higher do you have to jump than your colleagues with "traditional" backgrounds?

I propose an amendment to the CAP's plan: if a company is doing the work for which the trust exists, it is eligible for a tax credit. There are two components to this extension:

1. The company has implemented its own approved training program. The quality and nature of the program, as well as the student population being served and the salaries of the jobs for which they're destined are all approved by the aforementioned representative council.
2. The company has been certified by the council as an equitable employer. This is a check on toxic company culture, which is a driving factor in the steep attrition rate

among people of color in tech. No more training people for jobs at toxic companies and then asking them with a shrug to choose between their financial and mental wellness. It's time to expect both.

I don't have many regrets about the work we've done thus far at Resilient Coders, but one that looms large is the fact that our alumni are often launching their careers under managers that undervalue and undermine them until they're ultimately bullied out of their jobs. This is not an occasional misfortune. It's a rampant problem. Sometimes—and in my experience, nearly always—it's the managers who need to grow or go, not the alumni. And there's not a thing we can do as the training provider other than complain to our contacts at the company. We could blacklist that particular employer, and sometimes we do. But if we were to blacklist every company that engaged in this sort of toxic behavior, we wouldn't have enough partners to justify a bootcamp.

Giving a tax credit to participating employers might also help shift the profile of companies that are either taking advantage of outside training programs or conducting their own training as a way of leveling the playing field. There's an overrepresentation of food service, hospitality, and construction at the moment, perhaps due to the fact that on-the-job training is already normalized in those industries. That's just the standard pipeline; you don't get a bachelor's degree in carpentry; you apprentice. And it's not because carpentry is any easier than most programming jobs. Such a notion is a figment of tech's legacy of opportunity hoarding. Whatever the reason, we need to broaden the scope of options available to workers coming up through training programs by bringing tech to the table. It's indefensible economically, let alone morally, to shuttle trainees almost exclusively into industries that are either shrinking or leveling out, or that are most vulnerable to recession. Jobs in the country's fastest-growing industry—specifically its highest-paying careers, such as software engineering—must be available to those who have the ambition and inclination to pursue them.

As I touched on in chapter 4, government-sponsored apprenticeships are a relatively recent innovation in the context of software engineering. They represent a great example of both the benefits and limitations of publicly funded interventions. Several states are implementing programs through which to incentivize companies—including tech firms- -to hire from training providers. Models vary, but generally speaking, state-registered apprenticeships follow a set of core principles: First, an apprenticeship is a job. Apprentices are paid from the instant they begin their apprenticeship, and they are expected to continue into a full-time position, with a wage increase, when the apprenticeship ends. This is a departure from more traditional bootcamp models, in which companies pick and choose from graduates who have already finished their training. In the apprenticeship model, companies make a commitment to hire someone before the apprentice knows how to do the job.

Different models mitigate this risk in a variety of ways. Some apprenticeship firms issue standardized "logic" tests to applicants and skim their cohort of apprentices from the top. This requires faith in the idea that standardized tests can be indicative of someone's likely performance on the job and can be totally free of bias. Sometimes there is a "pre-apprenticeship" program, during which pre-apprentices gain some preliminary skills, and there's not necessarily a real commitment to usher them into a subsequent formal apprenticeship if they underperform.

Second, apprenticeships feature a combination of classroom learning and on-the-job learning, each with a required number of hours. On-the-job training is supported by a cohort of workplace mentors. Sometimes the proportion of apprentices to mentors is mandated by the state.

Third, there is some sort of financial incentive provided or supported by the state. Both the classroom training provider and the employer are compensated, typically through direct payments, capital grants, or tax credits.

Resilient Coders has been down this road a few times, exploring different apprenticeship models with different government agencies. We've really wanted to make it work. But it hasn't yet, for a few key reasons. We insist on retaining the autonomy to turn away candidates from White middle- or upper-class backgrounds, for the simple reason that they're just not who we work for. A couple of government agencies have been uncomfortable with our criteria for accepting applicants. They argue that a government that purports to represent all of us can't be seen picking and choosing candidates based on personal attributes such as their race. They can, however, exert considerable effort in promoting the opportunity in communities of color. So while we wouldn't be allowed to reject candidates based on their personal attributes, we would be allowed to actively seek out candidates based on their personal attributes.

We're simply not interested in engaging in an elaborate tea ceremony during which we purport to talk about race without ever talking about race. Subtlety is not our thing. The crisis in tech is explicitly racialized, and the solution must be explicitly racialized as well.

We have been approached to participate in a government-backed opportunity that was open to granting us complete autonomy over admissions. But that hasn't worked out either. And it hasn't worked for an interesting and unexpected reason: We ran a limited pilot, and none of the companies that participated in it cared about the $10,000 discount (subsidized by the state) for which they would be eligible if they worked with us specifically under the terms of the state-registered apprenticeship. Those that were already interested in hiring from Resilient Coders before joining the pilot program preferred to simply pay us the full fee we usually charge and be done with it. They were happy to forfeit the tax credit in the interest of keeping the relationship simple. The companies that hadn't necessarily been interested in hiring from us before the pilot program were no different. Whether they came into the conversation wanting to hire out of Resilient Coders or not, the offer of a discount on the fee swayed no one.

To be clear, the terms of the apprenticeship agreement were not onerous. There was no requirement in the apprenticeship model that extended significantly beyond what we already do without it. It required doing a minimal amount of paperwork, which our apprenticeship partners were ready and willing to walk the companies through, step by step. It required a commitment to slight tweaks in their employee onboarding process, such as formalizing a mentorship effort that should exist anyway when hiring an employee who is just starting their technical career. But we never even got to that level of granularity in our discussions. None of our companies even learned about those slight tweaks, because they turned down the terms of the state subsidy almost immediately.

This attitude presents an interesting challenge to the notion that financial incentives are the way to bring tech to the table. Maybe those companies don't care about discounts or tax relief schemes that amount to a few thousand dollars here or there because many of them are already flush with capital.

Suppose our experience is representative of a broader trend, and state-funded apprenticeships are not (yet) enough to move the industry. State agencies have come forward with a model and money, offering a path by which tech companies can offer on-the-job training. This should be what they want—tech is always complaining about a talent shortage. But then suppose the industry were to respond with a shrug, and then generally go back to business as usual, insisting on recruiting most—if not all—of their technical talent from expensive universities or from other companies. What if policy's not enough? What if it's a demand problem.

Does the tech industry even want any of this?

Policy matters. But culture matters more. Policies work best when they're in line with existing mainstream cultural values. They codify, support, protect, and even extend those values. But in those instances and contexts in which policies exist in opposition to the existing mainstream cultural values, the road is longer and harder. Consider the question of mask usage during the pandemic. In some cultural contexts, mask usage is nearly universal, because people believe that it is an effective way to keep them safe. And in others, mask usage is almost nonexistent, because people don't believe that it keeps them safe. Or rather, they believe in the authority of people who demonize mask usage. In some contexts, mask usage has evolved in step with the recommendations of the Centers for Disease Control (CDC), because people in those settings believe in following the science and in the CDC's authority to represent it. All of this is culture. Your relationship with facts is cultural.

Mandating more equitable recruitment and employment practices at the policy level may turn out to be a bit like asking rural White baby boomers to mask up: it needs to happen, but it must also be accompanied by a top-to-bottom overhaul of culture.

Can we agree?

During a moment of turbulence at Resilient Coders, in a conversation with Leon about disagreements among staff, he interrupted me to say, "Just be mad with us."

Some of our teammates were frustrated with me about the direction the company was taking during our expansion to new markets. They were worried that we could be abandoning our commitment to being the radically student-centric organization we purport to be. For example, we were choosing to allocate our resources to serving more students the same experience, rather than serving fewer students an even better experience. It seemed to them like treading too far down this path could take us toward the sort of industrial nonprofit model that we vocally oppose: Billions and billions served, but what they're served is actively causing harm. We're supposed to represent a departure from this. Do we still?

While the bootcamp scaled within Boston, so did my ambitions for the scope of our work. I wanted us to finally tackle all the systemic barriers that keep our graduates from unlocking their potential at a level that is commensurate with their skills. I saw a future for us in which we launched an advocacy effort parallel to our training. We might have worker centers that would function almost like a union in some respects. We could begin the work of orchestrating coordinated efforts among a network of organizations like ours. I was getting tired of constantly fitting our graduates into predominantly White spaces and abetting a system that expects them to assume one hundred percent of the burden of their cultural integration. I felt it was time for the burden to be distributed more fairly. I wanted us to change tech.

But we can't do all of that. After exploring these different avenues, I ultimately decided that Resilient Coders needs to do just one thing and do it exceptionally well: teach people to code and connect them with jobs as software engineers. There's something to be said for focus.

So we turned *away* from our aspirations to tackle systemic barriers before they'd even really begun. Instead, we expanded laterally. We took on more students without changing much about the program. Many of those students were uprooting their lives to enroll in the bootcamp. People quit jobs. They borrowed money to get by and suffered all manner of financial hardship during their time in the program, which is too intense to allow for a second job. Our students were showing up for Resilient Coders with everything they had. Was Resilient Coders showing up for them with the same level of urgency?

Some of the staff didn't think so. They were questioning the decision to expand the program and help more students rather than help fewer students more. I have my reasons for every decision I've ever made about the program, including this one, and I was sharing some of them with Leon during a tense conversation when he cut me off. "Stop trying to jump to solutions," he said. "Just be mad with us."

I don't know how to do that. I don't know how to be mad without offering solutions. Action is my love language.

"Can we agree that our stipend is not enough to live on?" he asked.

Yes, of course. It's not.

"Can we agree that sometimes we cause harm?"

Yes. We do. It's an intense program, and not everyone gets through it. No one gets out unscathed.

"Can we agree that all of this is fucked up?"

Yeah, it's fucked up. When you work for an organization like ours, you understand that you never do your people the justice that they actually deserve. You cannot create ideal scenarios; ideal is not an option. With an immense amount of work, you can create scenarios that are somewhat less unjust than the alternative. That's what we do: We mitigate unjust scenarios. Anything you do at an organization like ours is manifestly unworthy of the people for whom you do it. And this reality is itself unjust. It's also exhausting. Imagine going to work every day knowing that nothing you do that day will be enough.

This inescapable reality lay the groundwork for a collective lament that we needed to share as a group of humans who care deeply about a broader group of humans. Nothing we do will ever be adequate to the task at hand. It's impossible not to feel small in the face of a challenge so immense, daunting, and terrifying as the economic oppression of people you care about. All of us are exhausted. We're all burnt out and angry. But the act of naming it, taking a minute to just feel our anger together was somehow a relief from the heaviness of experiencing all of this in isolation. Just saying, "This sucks," and getting a nod from your colleagues is its own small bit of redemption. I had been trying to present a strategy when I should have started by presenting humanity.

To rebuild anything, first you must tear down. Once we had a sense of our core tenets, we could begin to ask ourselves rebuilding questions. Who *should* we be? What does that look like? How much of that is possible? What are we willing to sacrifice to get there? Every member of our team, for example, expressed a willingness to suffer layoffs if it meant we could double our stipends to our students.

And so began our process of overhauling the program, bit by bit. This would be our sixth major pivot as an organization in seven years. And that's by design. An organization that stops pivoting stops innovating.

"What's really wild," said Leon, "is that we actually have a shot at getting this right." This is the energy we bring to our self-disruption.

Can we agree that now is the time to tear down and rebuild?

Consider creating your own version of Google's "Ten things we know to be true" at your company or within a group of people who want to lead change. These items can be aspirational: Ten things that must become true.

Can we agree that wealth and race must cease to be factors in someone's ability to launch, sustain, and advance a career in tech? And that current efforts to abate this crisis are not working? I've been calling it a crisis, but I should ask: Can we agree that it's a crisis?

Can we agree that a company has a civic responsibility to its city? Can we agree that when a company fails to offset its own contribution to gentrification by hiring exclusively from White privileged communities, it's causing harm?

Don't try to jump to solutions right away or to give all the reasons why all of this is the way it is. Just be mad with me for a second.

Can we agree that free training is part of the solution?

Can we agree that Black Wages Matter too?

Can we agree that all of us in tech are in aggregate both the problem and the solution? I agree with Leon: We actually have a shot at getting this right. Who would we be if we didn't take that shot?

To our colleagues at other nonprofit workforce development organizations who must also be frustrated and daunted by their own smallness: I don't really have any new solutions for us, but I can offer you my own humanity. You have my solidarity, even if today all that really means in practice is that we sit in our respective cities, maybe operating in different contexts but experiencing similar frustrations. If we overlap in our feelings of concern for people we care about, that's something. It's a beginning, and it matters.

This is not a "solutions" book, because that's not where the scarcity is. We're not low on ideas. We're short on all the other things that are much harder to develop than ideas. We're short on time and energy. We're low on the sorts of shared experiences and perspectives that build up to unity. And we don't all agree on what economic justice is. Can we agree that whatever it looks like, we haven't seen it yet?

Can we agree that it's not just about putting people into jobs but about a broader recalibration of power? And that without working to recalibrate power what we are is a community of talent vendors? There's nothing wrong with being a talent vendor, if that's what you want to do. But that's not what's in my own soul. It's not why I do the work that I do.

Can we agree that each of us is too small to do anything?

Can we agree that we've turned other people's poverty into a business? We owe it to the people we serve to confront this fact and to never quite make peace with it.

Can we agree that the work we do is worthy of amplification and celebration and that we deserve to do both of these together? Can we take a minute to reflect on how powerful that would be? It's important to be angry together, but it's also important to make space for joy. Can we agree that experiencing joy together would somehow feel like an act of resistance in a system in which so many of us are competitors?

Can we agree that we need to find each other and develop a national network of organizations fighting for the same things? Can we agree that if we're ever successful—not with our individual programs but in the underlying missions for which our programs were created—that it will have been because we managed to organize around shared objectives?

We have a shot at getting this right. There is a version of the future in which we've won this particular fight for economic justice in tech, and there must be a thousand paths to it. But each of them will require a unity of purpose that we don't have yet. We will build up to it. Each of these paths involves a dramatic shift in tech culture. It's already begun. There will be legislative battles, for which we will organize and canvas. All of this is ahead of us, and we'll get to it. Solidarity is real to the extent that it manifests in action. But start with humanity. Be mad with us.

ACKNOWLEDGMENTS

FIRST OF ALL, I should note that when I'm shamelessly bragging about Resilient Coders, I'm bragging chiefly about other people's work. I've had the honor of working alongside some amazing people: Tyler, Kunle, Muigai, Helen, Leon, Stephanie, Rougui, Lexi, Adrianna, Nick, Flex, Atiya, Vonds, Ellie, Erica, and Ayanna. Thank you for making this organization what it is.

I write a lot about our Freireian pedagogy in this book. That's all Leon's influence and work. My contribution was getting out of his way.

Not only does this team make Resilient Coders better; it also makes me better at my job. I write a lot in this book about organized workers approaching their leadership from a position of power. I have actually been on the leadership side of that table. My own team at Resilient Coders has approached me in the past to challenge some of my decisions that they felt distracted us from our aspirations to be a radically student-centric organization. In so doing, they made the organization stronger and better. Stronger and better don't always go together. They do at Resilient Coders, and much of that is because of this team.

It's also largely because of our alumni. I write about our efforts to develop an active alumni community. That's not something I can do. We have amazing alumni who step up and make our community what it is.

Students and alumni are at the center of our community, but they're not the entirety of it. We have the benefit of having many supporters, volunteers, and progressive employers who make what we do possible. We have a board composed of activists who have worn many hats to fit whatever role was needed. They're my kitchen cabinet and the best line of defense against my own rash ideas. They are amazing human beings.

It was a Resilient Coders mentor, employer, and ally who connected me to Beacon Press, actually. Amanda Beiner was instrumental in getting this book off the ground. She even read early drafts of the first chapter. So did my friend and former colleague Shaula Clark. She was one of the editors at the *Boston Phoenix* and a no-brainer choice for me when I was trying to think of people whose opinions I would need early on. I like to think there's more than a little bit of the *Phoenix* running through these pages. I guess on some level I even wanted to make sure of it.

Great research isn't something you stumble across. My friend Angie Jaimez sent me several of the studies referenced in this book.

Shout out to my city. Boston is home to so many more revolutions and revolutionaries than those you read about in middle school. All we ever do out here is envision the future and then fight for it.

Special thanks to my amazing editor, Rachael Marks, who understood this book even better than I did at times. She's been instrumental in honing this book into the best version of itself. Thanks as well to the whole team at Beacon Press.

I want to acknowledge my friends, for sitting patiently through the tirades that would ultimately make up the bulk of the book and for egging me on. And beyond their roles in the development of this book, they've stuck with me through thick and thin. Thank you all.

Properly thanking my family would require its own chapter. In the context of this book, my parents are historically and socially conscious people who cared deeply about raising my sister and me in a way that kept us close to our family in Mexico, our heritage, and our culture. This would be a very different book without their influence. My extended family, including the family I married into, is "acknowledgeable" way beyond the context of this book. I would be a very different person without their influence. I'm a member of a big group of people who love effusively. Everything else about my life is a footnote to this one main point. That's my autobiography in two sentences.

And to Sarah, love of my life: It feels weird to thank you for your influence on this book, because I have so much more to be grateful for than your utility to me. So instead, I'll just say that the time I spend with you is consistently the highlight of my day, going all the way back to the moment you approached this random shady character in the laundry room to ask if he knew how to operate the washing machines. I stand by my answer, by the way. All you can ever really do is throw everything you've got into that thing, start it, and hope for the best. My final words of gratitude in this book go to Alma, my favorite thing about the future.

NOTES

CHAPTER 1: POWER CONSCIOUSNESS

1. Kimberly Clausing, *Open: The Progressive Case for Free Trade, Immigration, and Global Capital* (Cambridge: Harvard University Press, 2019).

2. Chuck Collins, "Updates: Billionaire Wealth, U.S. Job Losses and Pandemic Profiteers," Inequality.org, Institute for Policy Studies, May 6, 2022, https://inequality.org/great-divide/updates-billionaire-pandemic.

3. Shirley Leung and Larry Edelman, "Coronavirus Made the Wealth Gap Worse. How Long Can a Divided Economy Stand?" *Boston Globe*, September 5, 2020, https://www.bostonglobe.com/2020/09/05/business/coronavirus-made-wealth-gap-worse-how-long-can-divided-economy-stand/?s_campaign=breakingnews:newsletter.

4. Raj Chetty, John N. Friedman, Nathaniel Hendren, Michael Stepner, and the Opportunity Insights Team, "Job Losses Persist for Low-Wage Workers," Opportunity Insights Economic Tracker, Harvard and Brown Universities, April 1, 2022, https://www.tracktherecovery.org/.

5. William Darity Jr., Darrick Hamilton, Mark Paul, Alan Aja, Anne Price, Antonio Moore, and Caterina Chiopris. *What We Get Wrong About Closing the Racial Wealth Gap*, Samuel DuBois Cook Center on Social Equity and Insight Center for Community Economic Development, April 2018, https://socialequity.duke.edu/wp-content/uploads/2020/01/what-we-get-wrong.pdf.

6. Akilah Johnson, "That Was No Typo: The Median Net Worth of Black Bostonians Really Is $8," *Boston Globe*, December 11, 2017, https://www.bostonglobe.com/metro/2017/12/11/that-was-typo-the-median-net-worth-black-bostonians-really/ze5kxC1jJelx24M3pugFFN/story.html.

7. David Baboolall, Duwain Pinder, Shelley Stewart, and Jason Wright, *Automation and the Future of the African American Workforce*, McKinsey & Company, November 14, 2018, https://www.mckinsey.com/featured-insights/future-of-work/automation-and-the-future-of-the-african-american-workforce.

8. Alana Semuels, "Millions of Americans Have Lost Jobs in the Pandemic—and Robots and AI Are Replacing Them Faster Than Ever," *Time*, August 6, 2020, https://time.com/5876604/machines-jobs-coronavirus.

9. Anthony P. Carnevale, Tamara Jayasundera, and Artem Gulish, *America's Divided Recovery*, Georgetown University Center on Education and the Workforce, 2016, https://cew.georgetown.edu/cew-reports/americas-divided-recovery.

10. HackerRank, *2018 Student Developer Report*, https://www.hackerrank.com/research/student-developer/2018.

11. "America's New Aristocracy," *The Economist*, January 24, 2015.

12. Anthony P. Carnevale, Peter Schmidt, and Jeff Strohl, *The Merit Myth: How Our Colleges Favor the Rich and Divide America* (New York: New Press, 2020).

13. Anthony P. Carnevale, Megan L. Fasules, Michael C. Quinn, and Kathryn Peltier Campbell, *Born to Win, Schooled to Lose: Why Equally Talented Students Don't Get Equal Chances to Be All They Can Be*, Georgetown University Center on Education and the Workforce, 2019, https://cew.georgetown.edu/cew-reports/schooled2lose.

14. Debt Collective, *Can't Pay Won't Pay: The Case for Economic Disobedience and Debt Abolition* (Chicago: Haymarket Books, 2020).

15. Jeffrey P. Thompson and Gustavo A. Suarez, *Accounting for Racial Wealth Disparities in the United States*, Federal Reserve Bank of Boston, 2019, https://www.bostonfed.org/publications/research-department-working-paper/2019/accounting-for-racial-wealth-disparities-in-the-united-states.aspx.

16. Heather McGhee, *The Sum of Us: What Racism Costs Everyone and How We Can Prosper Together* (New York: One World, 2022), 44.

17. Stephen Burd, *Undermining Pell: How Colleges Compete for Wealthy Students and Leave the Low-Income Behind*, New American Foundation, 2013, https://files.eric.ed.gov/fulltext/ED595529.pdf.

18. Burning Glass Technologies and the Strada Institute for the Future of Work, *Permanent Detour: Underemployment's Long-Term Effects on the Careers of College Grads*, 2018. The report can be downloaded at https://stradaeducation.org/report/the-permanent-detour.

19. Burning Glass and the Strada Institute, *Permanent Detour*.

20. National Equity Atlas, Slide 10, Burning Glass Technologies, National Fund, https://nationalfund.org, accessed August 25, 2022.

21. To be clear, this vision of a meritocratic workforce is not enough. I'm not advocating for an economic system in which our worth and our right to shelter are predicated on work ethic. That's deeply wrong and has been explored at length in other books. I'm arguing that even within the context of a capitalist system, which is itself already inherently unjust, some people experience more dimensions of injustice than others.

CHAPTER 2: WORKFORCE DEVELOPMENT AS A RADICAL
ACT OF ECONOMIC LIBERATION

1. Martin Hägglund, *This Life: Secular Faith and Spiritual Freedom* (New York: Pantheon Books, 2019), 215.

2. Abbie Langston, Justin Scoggins, and Matthew Walsh, *Race and the Work of the Future: Advancing Workforce Equity in the United States*, National Fund for Workforce Solutions, November 12, 2020, https://nationalfund .org/learning-evaluation/publications/race-and-the-work-of-the-future.

3. Isaiah Berlin, *Two Concepts of Liberty* (Oxford: Clarendon Press, 1966).

4. Milton Friedman, with the assistance of Rose D. Friedman, *Capitalism and Freedom* (Chicago: University of Chicago Press, 1962).

5. Jay Gillen, *The Power in the Room: Racial Education Through Youth Organizing and Employment* (Boston: Beacon Press, 2019).

6. Gillen, *The Power in the Room.*

7. UTEC, "Our Mission," https://utecinc.org/our-mission.

8. Jessica Gordon Nembhard, *Collective Courage: A History of African American Cooperative Economic Thought and Practice* (University Park: Pennsylvania State University Press, 2014).

9. Marlize van Romburgh and Gené Teare, "Funding to Black Startup Founders Quadrupled in Past Year, But Remains Elusive," Crunchbase, July 13, 2021, https://news.crunchbase.com/news/something-ventured-funding -to-black-startup-founders-quadrupled-in-past-year-but-remains-elusive.

10. Elijah Megginson, "When I Applied to College, I Didn't Want to 'Sell My Pain,'" *New York Times*, May 9, 2021, https://www.nytimes.com /2021/05/09/opinion/college-admissions-essays-trauma.html.

CHAPTER 3: DISRUPTION OF SELF

1. John Adams to Abigail Adams, 18 February 1776, Founders Online, National Archives, accessed July 19, 2022, https://founders.archives.gov /documents/Adams/04-01-02-0229.

2. We tend to fetishize "boldness" in our culture, and we forget that it's just a gentler word for risky and unpopular decision-making. By definition, boldness will diminish as the pool of decision-makers grows, unless all of them share exactly the same background, perspective, and role.

3. Jason Fried and David Heinemeier Hansson, *Rework* (New York: Currency, 2010).

4. Pranshu Verma, "'Nothing Actually Changes': Boston Tech Workers of Color Blast the Sector's Attempts to Be Antiracist," *Boston Globe*, July 31, 2021.

CHAPTER 4: DISRUPTION OF INDUSTRY

1. William Darity Jr., Darrick Hamilton, Mark Paul, Alan Aja, Anne Price, Antonio Moore, and Caterina Chiopris, *What We Get Wrong About*

Closing the Racial Wealth Gap, Samuel DuBois Cook Center on Social Equity and Insight Center for Community Economic Development, April 2018, https://socialequity.duke.edu/wp-content/uploads/2019/10/what-we-get -wrong.pdf. Italics in original.

2. "Ta-Nehisi Coates Extended Interview," *The Daily Show*, December 13, 2016, https://www.cc.com/video/vbyz5z/the-daily-show-with-trevor -noah-exclusive-ta-nehisi-coates-extended-interview.

3. Assata Shakur, *Assata: An Autobiography* (Chicago: Lawrence Hill Books, 1987).

4. Heather McGhee, *The Sum of Us: What Racism Costs Everyone and How We Can Prosper Together* (New York: One World, 2021).

5. Frank Dobbin and Alexandra Kalev, "Why Diversity Programs Fail," *Harvard Business Review*, July–August 2016, https://hbr.org/2016/07/why -diversity-programs-fail.

6. David Harvey, "The 'New' Imperialism: Accumulation by Dispossion," Vol. 40: *Socialist Register 2004: The New Imperialist Challenge* 40, https://socialistregister.com/index.php/srv/article/view/5811.

7. Charles Tilly, *Durable Inequality* (Oakland: University of California Press, 1997).

8. Catherine Riegle-Crumb, Barbara King, and Yasmiyn Irizarry, "Does STEM Stand Out? Examining Racial/Ethnic Gaps in Persistence Across Postsecondary Fields," *Educational Researcher* 48, no. 3 (February 21, 2019): 133–44, https://doi.org/10.3102/0013189X19831006.

CHAPTER 5: YOU HAVE THE POWER TO BREAK THE DAM

1. Mediators Beyond Borders, "Conflict Literacy Framework," https:// mediatorsbeyondborders.org/what-we-do/projects/dpace/conflict-literacy framework.

CHAPTER 6: REBUILDING

1. Claude M. Steele, "Thin Ice: Stereotype Threat and Black College Students," *The Atlantic*, August 1999, https://www.theatlantic.com/magazine /archive/1999/08/thin-ice-stereotype-threat-and-black-college-students /304663/.

2. This quote has been widely attributed to Watson (b. 1940), a visual artist, activist, and educator, but she has refused to take sole credit for a slogan she says she helped create as part of an Aboriginal rights group that met in Queensland during the 1970s. See Miz Many Names, "Attributing Words," Unnecessary Evils blog, November 3, 2008, https://unnecessaryevils .blogspot.com/2008/11/attributing-words.html, and the Invisible Children website, https://invisiblechildren.com/blog/2012/04/04/the-origin-of-our -liberty-is-bound-together.

CHAPTER 7: BIG IDEAS

1. Liva Lam, "A Design for Workforce Equity: Workforce Redesign for Quality Training and Employment: A Framing Paper," Center for American Progress, October 16, 2019, https://www.americanprogress.org/article/design -workforce-equity.